The 'Open Councils' and the Islamic Concept Of Rule in Saudi Arabian Politics

Dr. Faisal bin Misha'al bin Sa'ud bin 'Abdul-'Aziz Al-Sa'ud

Published by
Gulf Centre for Strategic Studies

ISBN: 1 84051 015 3

Ibn Misha'al bin Sa'ud bin 'Abdul-'Aziz Al-Sa'ud, Faisal.
The "Open Councils" and the Islamic Concept of Rule in Saudi Arabian Politics
ISBN 1 84051 015 3

Copyright © 2003 Gulf Centre for Strategic Studies Ltd., London

All Rights Reserved. No part of this publication may be produced, stored in a retrieval system or transmitted in any form or by means, electronic, electrostatic, magnetic tape, mechanical photocopying, recording or otherwise without the permission in writing of the copyright holder.
ISBN: 1 84051 015 3

Gulf Centre for Strategic Studies
3rd Floor
46 Grays Inn Road
London WC1X 8LR
United Kingdom
Tel: 020 7430 1367
Fax: 020 7404 9025
Email: (IBM) gcss@btconnect.com
Bahrain: Villa No. 2768, Road 2442, Juffair, PO Box 11505, Bahrain
Tel: 00973 825600 Fax: 00973825700,
Email: (IBM) gcssbh@batelco.com.bh
Cairo: Flat 9, Second Floor, 6 Aisha Al Taymoreya St., Garden City, Cairo, Egypt.
Tel.: 00202 794 5949 Fax: 00202 792 3579
Email: (IBM) ggi@link.net

{Is it judgement from (the days of) ignorance that they are seeking? Who, for a people assured (in their belief), can give judgement better than Allah?}

The Holy Qur'an, Surat Al-Ma'idah: 50

Dedication

It gives me great pleasure to dedicate this comparatively small work to the founder of modern Saudi Arabia and the architect of its rise, the late King 'Abdul-'Aziz bin 'Abdur-Rahman Al-Faisal Al-Sa'ud and his faithful men (may Allah have mercy on them). Additionally, I dedicate it to all who witnessed, heard or read about the miracle of 'Abdul-'Aziz, and discovered his astounding achievements, who appreciated the secrets behind his success, victories and clear-sightedness, and who followed the deceased King's deeds and words.

Contents

Introduction VII
By His Royal Highness Prince Salman bin 'Abdul-'Aziz

Chapter One
Theoretical framework 1
1-1 Introduction 2
1-2 Saudi Arabian Governance 2
1-3 The Role of Islam in the Regime 5

Chapter Two
Sources of Information and Methodology of Collection 9
2-1 Foreword 10
2-2 Available References on Saudi Arabia 10
2-3 Personal Meetings 15
2-4 Questionnaire 16
2-5 Summary 16

Chapter Three
**The Kingdom of Saudi Arabia's Historical Background
and Geography** 17
3-1 Foreword 18
3-2 Geography of Saudi Arabia 18
3-3 The Administrative Provinces 19
3-4 Saudi Arabia's Historical Background 26
3-5 Summary 37

Chapter Four
The Religious and Cultural Basis of the Islamic State 39
4-1 Foreword 40
4-2 The Islamic Political Regime's Structure 40
4-3 The Authority of the Islamic State 42
4-4 The Kingdom of Saudi Arabia's Ruling System 42
4-5 The Tribal Model of the Arabian Peninsula 43
4-6 Summary 44

Chapter Five
International Comparisons 45
5-1 Foreword 46
5-2 Comparative Hypothesis 46
5-3 A View of the Relationship between the Type of Rule and the Saudi Style of Life 48
5-4 Analytical Comparisons 51
5-5 Summary 53

Chapter Six
The Open Councils:
Procedures and Functions 55
6-1 Foreword 56
6-2 The Concept of the Council 56
6-3 The History of the Council 56
6-4 The Organisational Structure of Saudi Arabia's Government 57
6-5 The Open Council's Effectiveness: An Interview with the Emir of Riyadh 63
6-6 The Results of the Field Study 66
6-7 Summary 68

Chapter Seven
Results and Expectations 69
7-1 Results 70
7-2 Expectations 72

Bibliography 74

Appendices 77
Appendix 1: A note circulated by the Custodian of the two Holy Mosques when he was a deputy of the Prime Minister, concerning the importance of the 'open door' policy. 78
Appendix 2: The Law of the Shura Council 79
Appendix 3: The Questionnaire 92
Appendix 4: The Law of the Provinces 94
Appendix 5: The Basic Law of Government 102
Appendix 6: The Cabinet System 112

Figures

Fig. 1 A map of the Administrative Provinces of Saudi Arabia 19
Fig. 2 The political system during King 'Abdul-'Aziz's era 34
Fig. 3 Development of practical and political measures for the Open Councils 35
Fig. 4 A comparison between the features of the West's system of government and the characteristics of the Kingdom of Saudi Arabia's ruling system 48
Fig. 5 The restrictions on the Saudi Monarchy 50
Fig 5a A comparison of Arab and Western government (J. Mateka Ph.D.) 51
Fig. 6 The Minister's Council of Saudi Arabia 59
Fig. 7 The formation and levels of the Council 61

Introduction

By His Royal Highness Prince Salman bin 'Abdul –'Aziz

Praise be to Allah and the Lord's Blessings and Peace upon Our Prophet Muhammad, His family and companions.

King 'Abdul-'Aziz bin 'Abdur-Rahman Al-Sa'ud and his sons the Kings after him, used the policy of "Open Doors". It can be considered a method of rule based on the teachings of the Holy Qur'an, the example of the Prophet Muhammad (Peace be upon Him), and a way of promoting the relationship between the ruler and the ruled.

The successful achievement of these policy goals is - after Allah's help - due to the devotion to Islam by Saudi Arabia's leaders and people. Additionally, the late King 'Abdul-'Aziz established exemplary methods of rule, to be examined in this work, which have been preserved excellently by his offspring, including the current Custodian of the Two Holy Mosques (may Allah protect him).

Furthermore, this book - "The 'Open Councils' and the Islamic Concept of Rule in Saudi Arabian Politics" - authored by our dear son Faisal ibn Misha'al bin Sa'ud bin 'Abdul-'Aziz Al Sa'ud, analyses in detail the nature of the Open Councils inside Saudi Arabia, revealing them as a real method for uniting the people and their leaders. It shows these open meetings to be a useful opportunity for the exchange of opinion for the sake of Islam, the raising of the state, its stability, and peace.

I pray to Allah, the Almighty, to support this peaceful Kingdom for the welfare of this righteous religion, all its followers, and this country.

Finally, praise be to Allah. The Lord's Blessings and Peace be upon our Prophet Muhammad.

Prince Salman bin 'Abdul-'Aziz
Governor of Riyadh's Administrative district

Preface

Thanks to the only God and Allah's Blessing and Peace be upon the Last Prophet Muhammad bin 'Abdullah.

This book started out as a postgraduate thesis at California State University, Tchico in 1408 AH / 1988 AD.

In 1406 AH / 1986 AD, while I was attending an intensive course in English Language at Washington University's Institute in Seattle, an English language teacher asked a Saudi student about the form of government in Saudi Arabia. The Saudi youth hesitated before answering, then with unjustified shyness he said, "we have a monarchy". There were many students in that class who belonged to republican countries, including Americans, who assumed republican states were the ideal and took a cynical view of monarchies.

It is worth mentioning that after the lesson had finished, I talked to the young man. Consequently, I came to the conclusion that the young man was ashamed of anything related to monarchy inside the USA, as if it were a horrible crime. At that moment, I felt rather bitter. I wished I could have responded to such charges and proudly defended my country and Islam on the terms of Americans' own culture. After all, my nation, its regime, heritage and marvellous culture are something for all Muslims and Saudis to be proud of.

Later on, when I was wandering in a Saudi library, I came across a book entitled "The Foreign Policy of the Kingdom of Saudi Arabia" written by Dr 'Abdullah Al-Qabba' in 1406 AH/1986 AD. Two things attracted my attention: firstly, its topic, and secondly, a professor of mine at King Sa'ud University was its author. Upon reading one of its chapters, I found a detailed discussion about the Open Councils as a key instrument of decision making in the Kingdom of Saudi Arabia (KSA). However, I found this issue to be in need of more scientific and practical research. For this reason, it was chosen as the subject of my MA thesis.

This issue occupied all of my attention, as I felt that it had not been dealt with effectively before. In addition, Western intellectuals still needed to be informed about many aspects of Open Councils in Saudi Arabia, as well as the unique and spontaneous relation between ruler and ruled and its relationship to Arab and Islamic heritage.

My MA research was an opportunity to introduce this subject, supported by authentic references that clarify this issue and shed light on aspects of KSA that may be difficult to understand.

Many people had expected me to face great obstacles in obtaining the required references. But Allah helped his hardworking slave overcome these difficulties.

For truth and history, the support of His Royal Highness, Governor of Riyadh District, Prince Salman bin 'Abdul-'Aziz had a great impact on me. He had opened his heart before his office, encouraged and helped me in my study, agreeing to meet with me despite his busy schedule as a Governor of the home capital receiving a large number of different people since he had been appointed. His support included a public opinion poll, for one week, among Riyadh Governor's residents about the Open Councils.

This work has taken ten years to reach the publication stage. Not all academic studies are suitable for reproduction as a book; consequently, it has been rearranged to render it universally accessible.

A further reason delaying preparation of this book is that it is my first work. I take full responsibility for everything in it. I have a grave responsibility before Allah the Almighty and the late King, in addition to the field of specialisation that I have ventured to tackle. The publication of this book has been delayed by my inability to find time to edit it for so many reasons that I do not wish the reader to be concerned with.

Encouragement by many friends and some specialists has been the real motivation in bringing this work into the public domain. I pray to my Lord that this study will be a worthwhile contribution to the field, and that all those concerned with the issues here will find some benefit in it.

Fortunately, the delay in preparing this book has enabled me to find out in detail about the 'Last Basic Ruling Systems'[1], issued in 1413 AH/1993 AD. This publication has helped clarify my vision about the system of rule in Saudi Arabia.

The importance of this book is that it is the first academic research that deals with Open Councils as a basic characteristic of monarchy in Saudi Arabia. This study also compares monarchy guided by Islam and secular monarchical regimes.

It is not my intention to denigrate republican democracies or argue that Saudi Arabia is more democratic than they are. Rather, my intention is to contribute to the dialogue among cultures, and to explain that the practice of democracy in Saudi Arabia is different from that practised in the West due to the cultural and religious differences between Saudi Arabia and Western Countries.

Finally, I pray to Allah to make this work useful for everyone who reads it. So, if it is right, it is from Allah. But, if it is wrong, it comes from me. May the Lord direct us to the Right Path!

Riyadh 1/9/1420 AH

* For further information, please write to the author at this address:
H.R.H. Prince Faisal bin Misha'al bin Abdul Aziz Al-Saud
P.O. Box: 90.000
Riyadh 11692
Kingdom of Saudi Arabia.

---

[1] Royal Decree #A/13, 3/3/1414 H

A note about transliteration from Arabic to English

I have used one of the standard conventions of transliteration from Arabic to English throughout the book. However, there are some inconsistencies where proper names are mentioned due to their widespread or chosen use with a particular spelling in English. I have also avoided representing the long vowels present in Arabic in order to simplify matters.

Chapter One

Theoretical Framework

1-1: Introduction
1-2: Saudi Arabian Governance
1-3: The Role of Islam in the Regime

1-1 Introduction

Saudi Arabia was classed as a third world state until the late 1960s. It has developed a great deal since its foundation, especially in the last quarter of the twentieth century (between 1390 to 1420 AH) and it has successfully implemented six 5 Year Development Plans.

Many observers believe that crude oil stands behind the spectacular development of Saudi Arabia. Admittedly oil is an important natural resource that has played a significant role in the process of development up until now. However, there are other important factors to be taken into consideration. The most prominent of these are the stable political environment in Saudi Arabia and its safe society. Both of these factors stem from the application of Islamic laws based on the Holy Qur'an and the *Sunnah*[1] of the Prophet Muhammad (Peace be upon Him), as the constitution of the country. Furthermore, the leadership is faithful to the country as well as to Islam.

To understand the successful development of Saudi Arabia one needs to understand the nature of the state, its powerful elements, its properties, its strong political atmosphere and the application of Islamic faith. This book "The Open Councils" intends to deal with these issues.

1-2 Saudi Arabian Governance

The Kingdom of Saudi Arabia (KSA) has a unique position among Islamic countries because the two most sacred Islamic cities, Mecca and Medina, are within her territories. For this reason, the Saudi King, government and people feel that there are special obligations incumbent upon them not only towards these two holy towns but also towards other sacred Muslim sites as well as the preservation of Islam.

Legislation derived from the Holy Qur'an and the sacred Sunnah is the basis of everyday life in the Saudi Kingdom. The Kingdom considers itself a natural extension of traditional Islamic government in which a Caliph was accepted by the people as head of state. In spite of the fact

---

[1] The *Sunnah* refers to the Prophet Muhammad's practices and sayings, which supplement the teachings of the holy Qu'an in Islamic law.

that this system of government was historically prevalent in all Muslim countries, it changed over time due to outside influences, such as colonisation, partition and secular republican movements.

In any human society the form of governance is the result of interaction between the history, geography, society, economy, and traditions of the regime. This is true for KSA as well. Saudi government has developed along with the cultural, social and economic progress of Saudi Arabian society through the application of Islamic principles.

We should emphasise that the Saudi system has to be considered within the framework of Islamic religion, not only because Saudis are Muslims, but also because Saudi rule depends on Islamic *Shari'a* (the code of law based on the Holy Qur'an and the Sunnah). This allows the needs and rights of all people to be fulfilled completely[2].

Rule in the Saudi Kingdom is considered to be a system of Monarchy based on the Islamic principle of *Shura* (consultation). Government relies on Islamic laws based on the Qur'an and the Sunnah. Thus, this form differs from other monarchical regimes that derive their constitutions from man-made legislation[3].

A crucial ingredient of Saudi Arabia's regime is the Open Councils, which are derived from the system of Islamic Shura. In an open council, Saudi officials meet publicly with the citizens to solve the people's problems. The concept of council, which, in this context, means the open meeting, will be explained in detail in the following chapters.

The King[4], his Crown Prince, the Second Deputy Prime Minister, the Interior Affairs Minister, and governors of the provinces hold open meetings to attempt to solve citizens' problems. I will argue that these gatherings, where rulers discuss freely with ordinary people, offer an

---

[2] Assah, Ahmed. *Miracle of the Desert Kingdom* (London: Johnson Publications, 1969 A.D) p. 151.

[3] Dahlan, Ahmed. *A Research into Saudi Arabia's Internal Policy* (Jeddah: Al-Shurouk Publication House, 1984 AD) p. 139.

[4] The King of Saudi Arabia is also the Prime Minister. (See Apendix 5, p.107.)

example of 'direct democracy' at work in Saudi Arabia. The system is considered (at least inside the Kingdom - in view of society's historical and religious composition) as better than a parliamentary system because of its intrinsic benefit to the Saudi people.

In the late 1970s, the Palestinian intellectual, Professor Edward Said, introduced the concept of 'Orientalism', which fundamentally challenged the way the West viewed the East. The term refers to the intellectual complex that informs the prejudices of Western-educated persons against Oriental societies. Said says that Orientalism is a mindset stemming from the idea of European cultural superiority over non-European peoples and this has been a powerful political force in the world. He describes it as "a Western style for dominating, restructuring and having authority over the Orient"[5]. Many hold that in a post-colonial world, this complex continues to marginalise Oriental cultural and political norms in the media, academia and through education.

In her research "Orientalism, Occidentalism and the Control of Women", Laura Nader, lecturer in anthropology at Berkeley University, C.A., finds that the Orientalist complex leads to devaluation of women in both Eastern and Western societies[6]. Her main assertion is that the same dichotomous logic behind Orientalists' misconceptions about the kinds of rule in the Orient, also leads to a perception of the status of women as inferior to that of men.

Many Western observers and analysts have propagated a negative image of Oriental states that do not follow democracy of the Western type. Similarly, the status and condition of women in the Orient has been severely criticised. Yet being culturally subjective, such judgements often distort the reality of Oriental societies, ignoring their numerous advantages.

That there is little information about "The Open Councils" in Western authors' writings is, in itself, evidence of this distortion. It appears that the lack of information about Arabs and Muslims has allowed people in Western societies to generalise unjustly about them. So, in writing this

---

[5] Said, Edward. *Orientalism* (New York, Random House, 1979 A.D.) pp. 3, 6, and 7

[6] Nader, Laura. " *Orientalism, Occidentalism, and the Control of Women*" (Paper Presented at Harvard University, March 1988 A.D).

book, I will try my best to prove that, inside KSA, there is a practical alternative to democracy, which suits Saudi Arabia's idiosyncrasies. I do not intend to claim that Saudi Arabia is more authentically democratic than Western countries. What is important, is to explain the differences and ask each side to understand and respect the culture of others.

1-3 The Role of Islam in the Regime

The whole of Saudi life is controlled by Islam according to Allah's words: {**whoso judgeth not by that which Allah hath revealed: such are disbelievers**} Al – Ma'idah: 50.

Islam is the foundation of modern Saudi society. Saudi Arabia's constitution is the Muslims' Holy Book, together with the Sacred Sunnah. This has been stated in Saudi Arabia's recently promulgated Basic Government Law.

To fully understand the nature of Saudi society, it is worth mentioning that Saudi Arabians see Muhammad (PBUH), as their only supreme leader. It is also important to understand that Islamic faith is life's framework in a way that may not be appreciated by Western nations. Islam is the basis of daily life of ordinary Saudis. For Saudi society, belief is everything. Therefore, Saudi Arabia has no need for a formal constitution because she relies on Islamic principles. The late King 'Abdul-'Aziz bin Sa'ud said, "our constitution is the Holy Qur'an as well as the Sunnah"[7]. His two succeeding sons, Kings Sa'ud and Faisal, also reiterated, "Saudi Arabia is an Islamic Arab sovereign country. The Qur'an and the Prophet's Sunnah are its only constitutions. All Saudi legislation is based on this truth"[8].

Consequently, Saudi leaders believe in the Shari'a as the source of all laws concerning life as a whole. They take pride in obeying the Holy Qur'an and the Sunnah. Some Muslim scholars claim that Islamic law has been used as a model by the lawmakers of other states: In the Napoleonic epoch, Islam influenced the French constitution

---

[7] Al-Oheideb, 'Abdul-'Aziz. *Phenomenon of Security during King 'Abdul-'Aziz's Reign* (Riyadh, Al-Isha'a Printing Shop, 1977 A.D.) p. 126.

[8] Dahlan, Ahmed. *op. cit.*, p. 127.

tremendously. Some years ago, the late King Faisal said: "If we wish to work for the welfare of our country, we do not need to import legislation from the outside. On the contrary, other states make use of Islamic laws. In Egypt, Napoleon issued Islamic laws after he had met the 'Ulama"[9].

It has been proven that Napoleon used Islamic rules in establishing his political policies, as well as in drafting the French Constitution. The French constitution in turn was widely studied by many countries when forming their own. Therefore, the application of Shari'a is absolutely vital to the Saudi rulers. Consequently, on every public occasion, they remind the audience to follow Islam completely.

The late King Faisal (may Allah have mercy on him) emphasised this point, saying, "first and foremost, our policy is based on the Holy Qur'an and the Sunnah of the Prophet. And the decisions we make are in accordance to our faith. All of our interests are defined by the Holy Qur'an and Sunnah".[10]

The Shari'a contains a code for the whole of life. It suits every time and place, which contrasts with the formal constitutions of other states. The unchangeable nature of Shari'a is the only reason that makes Saudi Arabia's Islamic rule, by Allah's Will, permanent across the ages. In this context, King Fahd stressed that "the main pillar of the Saudi Kingdom's political form is Islamic law derived from Holy Qur'an as well as the Sunnah"[11].

Similarly leaders of the nation are duty-bound to administer their country's affairs according to Shari'a. In Muslim's book of *Hadith*, Allah's Prophet, (PBUH), is reported to have said, "every man is a guardian. And, simultaneously, he is fully responsible for those in his guardianship"[12].

---

[9] *Ibid.*, p.137. NB. The *'Ulama* are the learned ones, entrusted with matters of law and religious teaching

[10] *Ibid.*, p.137.

[11] *Ibid.*, p. 138.

[12] Muslim bin al-Hajjaj al-Nisapuri, 'Abul-Husain. Sahih Muslim – a collection of the reports (*ahadith*) of the Prophet Muhammad's sayings and doings (*sunnah*) compiled in the 3rd Century AH.

Justice is the foundation of Governance

Since the establishment of the Saudi dynasty, Saudi leaders do their best to portray Islamic rule "as the best solution for humanity's problems. This proves as false the idea that religion must be separated from the state, and the claims that it prevents development"[13]. For their part, the Saudi nation is obliged to obey its leaders, for it is mentioned in Holy Qur'an. Allah says: **{O you who believe! Obey Allah, and obey the messenger and those who are in authority among you}** An-Nisa':59.

In this book, we shall see that the Islamic concept of rule is different from the Western one. Instead of looking at rule as a type of totalitarianism, Islamic rule focuses its efforts on humility. Experienced Saudi officials attempt to practice this. Monarchy, as a system of governance, has been frequently criticised in American intellectual circles. Either Americans have little information about Saudi Arabia's regime or they deliberately distort the picture. But, for the Saudi thinker, a different history is apparent.

Monarchy is a method of rule that offers a real example of the advanced Islamic way of life. As the late King Faisal said,

> "The title given by someone to a specified regime is just an ordinary name. But, what is significant here is the nature of the relationship between the leader and the citizen as well as the benefits offered by the system to its people. At present, there are many democracies all over the world, which vary in levels of success. But this situation does not apply to monarchical regimes; there is a single monarchy (Saudi Kingdom) that has brought progress to the Saudis. Consequently, the correct evaluation of any political system ought to be based on its achievements and not the title applied to it"[14].

The broader, Muslim society of KSA believe that the nation's leader will apply the Holy Qur'an's doctrines: **{Allah doth command you...if ye judge between people, that ye judge justly }** An-Nisa': 58.

---

[13] Al-Faisal, Khalid: *The Development And An Eyewitness* (Abha, Mazen Press, 1419 AH) pp. 26, 27.

[14] Khadduri, Majid. *Arab Contemporaries, The Roles of Personalities in Politics* (Baltimore: John Hopkins University Press, 1973 A.D).

The Open Councils

This desire to uphold Islamic principles and way of life has been deepened. So much so that the Council of Minister's Decree No. (693), 4-5/7/1389 AH, that organised Saudi Arabia's first development plan, states in its first article that "preserving religious and moral values is the most important target"[15].

The Shura process is also considered one of the basic tenets of Islam with respect to rule. It is mentioned in the Holy Qur'an:

{**It was by the mercy of Allah that thou wast lenient with them (O Muhammad), for if thou hadst been stern and fierce of heart they would have dispersed from round about you. So pardon them and ask forgiveness for them and consult with them upon affairs (of the moment). And when you have resolved (matters), then put your trust in Allah for Allah loves those who put their trust (in Him)**} Al-'Imran: 159.

Moreover, in the chapter of the Holy Qur'an entitled 'Ash-Shura' (Consultation), we find listed the behaviour that makes one deserving of the eternal rewards of Allah. It specifies that, amongst other things, such persons should be {**those... who conduct their affairs by mutual consultation**} Ash-Shura: 38. For this reason King 'Abdul-'Aziz's belief in this Islamic principle led him to form the Shura Council on 21/2/1345 AH (1925 AD). In 1346 AH (1926 AD), it was reorganised. Then, in 1347 AH (1927 AD), its by-laws were drawn up. This assembly lasted until the establishment of the ministers' cabinet in 1373 AH (1953 AD)[16].

As clarified in a circular issued by King Fahd when he was Crown Prince as well as Deputy Prime Minister, every Minister has a duty to publicly meet the people to help solve their problems. "All officials must, for at least one hour a day, have meetings with the ordinary citizens from their administered areas to solve their obstacles and identify the weaknesses of the state", he said[17]. This is the essence of democracy and it is the willing to serve the state and the people (see Appendix No. 1).

---

[15] Al-Faisal, Khalid. *op. cit.*, p. 37).

[16] Kingdom of Saudi Arabia, The Ministers' Council, The Circular Note No. 1 / 223, Riyadh: The Cabinet of Ministers Press. 1981 A.D

[17] Kingdom of Saudi Arabia, The Ministers' Council, The Circular Note No. 1 /223, Riyadh: The Cabinet of Ministers Press. 1981 A.D

The Open Councils

Chapter Two

Sources of Information and Methodology Of Collection

2 - 1: Introduction
2 - 2: Available References on Saudi Arabia
2 - 3: Personal Meetings
2 - 4: Questionnaire
2 – 5: Summary

2-1 Foreword

This chapter explains in detail the sources and references concerning Saudi Arabia's ruling system, and specifically the 'open door' policy. In addition, it describes the methods employed in the collection of information about the Open Councils.

2-2 Available References on Saudi Arabia

Open councils that gather the citizens and the leaders together are both an old and a new institution in Saudi Arabia. Although it is deeply rooted in early Islamic history, it is still active and alive in modern Saudi society. It is useful to consider what other authors have written about the history, nature, and socio-political significance of the Open Councils.

George Lipsky gave us a general description of the way in which the Open Council functions, when he said, "in his guests' tent, the Sheikh of the tribe holds an open council everyday. In these meetings, tribal men discuss substantial questions, because they are accustomed to go to the council daily to hold frank discussions with the Sheikh. But, if they are incapable of resolving any conflicts, such conflicts will be passed on to higher local levels or to the highest governmental level"

Later on, in the same book, Lipsky explains the Shura's cultural bases, which are fundamental to Islamic rule, he says, "[a] basic condition for a monarchical regime is the practice of Shura among its members. This condition arises from the tradition applied among the family's males and it is widespread in the Arabian Peninsula. Thus, in this culture, the Open Council is considered as one of the political customs".

Lipsky also says, "the Principle of Shura is an integral part of the methods used by the Sheikh of the Tribe in rule; he does not make a decision without consulting the tribe's elders as well as 'Ulama (scholars of Islamic law) if they are present" [18].

---

[18] Lipsky, George A. *Saudi Arabia: Its Society, Its Culture* (New Haben: H.R.A.F Press, 1959 A.D), pp. 77, 97 and 128

1) In his book "Saudi Arabia: Its Founding and Development", Muhammad Iqbal discusses an ordinary Saudi citizen's access to the top decision-makers. He concludes that any ordinary citizen can come to the Open Council. "Realising the necessity of meeting everyone" writes Iqbal, "King 'Abdul-'Aziz has worked hard to improve the principle of meeting between the ruler and his people. Now everybody is able to attend the Monarchical council in order to inquire about something or to give advice to his ruler."[19]. Thus, in the modern Open Councils of KSA, Iqbal argues that we have in place a mechanism that truly puts the power in the hands of the people.

In Saudi Arabia, the Open Council is now the foundation of governance. King Fahd has stressed in a press interview "my doors are open to all people". He has also encouraged the princes in Saudi Arabia to solve the problems of citizens quickly. He says, "princes of the provinces must not shirk their responsibilities towards their people; the officials as well as myself are in service of the citizens"[20].

As a practical example of this principle, 'Assir's Governor, Prince Khalid Al-Faisal, says, "from the first day, I regularly meet people openly in the morning, at the Centre of The Emirate. I start my work with joining the Open Council, as other Governors of the areas used to, to meet people and to listen to their problems. Citizens sit in front of my little table to open their hearts to me. I resolve their problems. In addition, I listen to the women's complaints by means of their special room's door, before going to the council of men"[21].

In his article, "Connecting Democracy with the System of Open Council", published in "Saudi Arabia Today", Peter Hopday says, " if there is a true democracy in this world, it is the KSA's system; for us democracy lies in the direct contact between the Head of the State and its ordinary citizen. So in Saudi Arabia everyone is able to meet the King freely"[22].

---

[19] Iqbal, Muhammad. *Saudi Arabia: Its Founding and Development* (Kashmir: Jagowal Printing Press, 1986 A.D) p. 74.

[20] King Fahd: *My door is open for everybody*, Arab News Newspaper, Issue Dt. 20/1/1988 A.D).

[21] Al - Faisal, Khaled. *op. cit.*, p. 60.

[22] Hopday, Peter. *Saudi Arabia Today* (London: Macmillan Press, 1986 A.D) p. 67.

Justice is the foundation of Governance

Here the question is: Is the Open Council purely an Arab monarchical institution? Or can it be described as an aspect of democratic rule? Writers have responded variously to this question. Naser Rashid and Esber Shaheen have treated the Open Council as a democratic tradition by saying that every man is free to attend the Open Council in order to represent his interests in person. "This democratic practice has been customary since the reign of King 'Abdul-'Aziz" they say, quoting the Governor of Riyadh, Prince Salman, who said to one of his Open Council guests, "anybody is in the position to reach any ruler in order to seek justice" [23].

Certain Western authors have argued that the Open Council does not fulfil the West's criteria for democracy. In his book, "Society and Economy in Saudi Arabia", Tim Niblock says, " in his daily Open Council, the meeting of the people with their King is described by observers as a democratic mode. But, this is incorrect; expressing opinions to the decision maker does not equal participation in adopting resolutions" [24]. And, in his book, "Saudi Arabia: Its Society, Its Culture", George Lipsky says: "The West's representative establishments do not occur in K.S.A. Nevertheless, putting into action the Open Councils at all levels, is common in this Kingdom" [25].

In his book, "The Foreign Policy of The Kingdom of Saudi Arabia", Dr. 'Abdullah Al-Qabba' argues that: "Saudi public opinion is voiced by modern mass media. The King and other officials attend the Open Councils to solve the people's complaints. And, every Tuesday, the King meets 'Ulama as well as other literates to exchange points of view concerning internal and external affairs. In addition to the above mentioned, he regularly meets Sheikhs of the Tribes and other persons"[26].

---

[23] Rashid, Naser. & Shaheen, Esber. *King Fahd and Saudi Arabia's Great Evolution* (Joplin, Mo: International Institute of Technology, 1987 A.D).

[24] Niblock, Tim. *State, Society and Economy in Saudi Arabia* (New York: St. Martin's Press, 1988 A.D) p. 89.

[25] Lipsky, *op. cit.,* p. 105.

[26] Al-Qabba', 'Abdullah. *The Foreign Policy of The Kingdom of Saudi Arabia*

The Open Councils

Justice is the foundation of Governance

At present, it is tradition to invite many citizens to dine with the King every week in order to discuss and resolve matters with him. This custom is unique in the world.

The Custodian of the Two Holy Mosques, King Fahd bin 'Abdul-'Aziz used to hold open meetings with academic professors as well as university students. During these meetings, domestic and foreign policies were discussed with the King and he would then take questions. Furthermore, many Princes, including the Crown Prince, Second Deputy Prime Minister, and Minister of the Interior receive people everyday seeking to overcome their difficulties.

Others have questioned whether such a council is fit for modern Saudi Arabia. In the handbook, "Saudi Arabia: A Country Study", issued by the U.S. Department of the Army, it has been reported:

> "Although most petitions submitted in the Open Council are personal, the ordinary people manage to talk about anything except attacking Islam. The Information Minister named this method of rule, which is characterised by focusing on things of personal significance, as "the Arab Democracy". It was effective during King 'Abdul-'Aziz's reign. However, with the progress of modernisation, this conventional council has seemed less active than before. The consultative organisation that strengthens if not replaces the Open Council in order to extend the principle of Shura is called The Shura Council. It is this authority that contains the intellectuals and highly efficient specialists. They are carefully selected to contribute, internally and externally, to political decision-making"[27].

Such claims of decline are often put forward outside KSA. Yet, inside

---

[Riyadh: Al-Farazdaq Press, 1986 A.D], p. 156.

[27] *Area Handbook, Saudi Arabia: A Country Study* [Washington D.C.: Headquarters, Department of The army, 1984 A.D], p.228.

The Open Councils

the Saudi Kingdom, attitudes towards the Open Council seem to be positive. In a lecture: "Saudi Arabia: State, Society and Economy" given by Prince 'Abdullah Al-Sa'ud, he said: "Western journalists and intellectuals frequently put forward questions concerning whether economic development in Saudi Arabia could lead to the decay of the traditional establishments. And sometimes, it is claimed that when the Kingdom has become more bureaucratic, the convention of the Open Council, which emphasises the direct contact between people and their leadership, will be subject to weakness. But, let me assure you that the Open Council still plays a very prominent role in our life"[28].

In his PhD dissertation entitled "The Legislative Process and Development of Saudi Arabia", Hamad Al-Hamad states, "a major aspect of the legal laws' effectiveness is that they are perceived to be the People's Sacred Laws. As a result, there is a spontaneous balance between state and its people, because functions of the state depend on Shari'a. Consequently, the political system is stabilised"[29].

If the term 'democracy' is considered to be a first principle of government, it can be defined as 'the government of the people by the people'. In this case, it differs from Shari'a, for Allah is the only Supreme Ruler of His slaves. Thus, democratic standards in this sense would seem unfair criteria by which to assess Saudi Arabia's rich Islamic-based development. If we want to evaluate a human society's political and cultural progress, it is inappropriate to apply imported ideologies from societies, which do not resemble the subject of our analysis historically, socially, scientifically or religiously.

The observer has a right to note that, in most underdeveloped countries, including some Arab and African states, democracy is employed as a slogan, propaganda, and the will of the government. When elections take place, it is insufficient; the Head of State continues to cling on to

---

[28] Al-Sa'ud, 'Abdullah. *"State, Economy, and Economy inside K.S.A"*, the *introductory remarks in the forum of "Saudi Arabia's Economy and Rule"* [The Arabian Gulf Studies centre, July / 1980 A.D].

[29] Al-Hamad, Hamad Sadun. *"The Legislative Process and The Development of Saudi Arabia"* [Ph.D. Diss. University of South Carolina. 1973 A.D], p. 187.

Justice is the foundation of Governance

power, making only a few cosmetic changes to his administration. That kind of 'democratic' procedure is a mask that only allows the achievement of short range and ineffectual policies.

However, KSA, as an Islamic country containing the two Holy Mosques and the homeland of Islam, has not violated her Islamic doctrines by importing foreign principles and pressing them on the people, who completely differ from other nations. As a result, King Fahd bin 'Abdul-'Aziz, who came into power in 1402 AH (1982 AD), and Saudi Arabia's leadership have pledged to develop the principle of Shura under a modern Islamic regime, which it is thought suits the Saudi people best.

In fact, in 1412 AH (1992 AD), a Shura system among reformist administrative rules was established after a careful study that made modern Saudi Arabia proud (see Appendix No. 2). But, it does not aim to supersede the Open Councils, which are a significant basis of the Saudi regime. This system is better than other countries' parliaments. In the Open Councils the rulers and the ruled meet face to face, there is no intermediate such as an MP, and questions are dealt with easily. So, it produces noticeable results. Two of which are:

1. When any state official is aware that a citizen can openly meet with him, the King, the Crown Prince, or others, the citizen will be treated justly.
2. Meeting the Head of the State pleases the citizen, whether the results are good or bad. The citizen feels that the leader cares for him, especially if he lives in a remote region.

Thus, we see that Saudis as well as their rulers are accustomed to the Open Councils, which are an organic part of their day-to-day life.

2-3 Personal Meetings

I have met two of Californian Berkeley University's professors for discussion concerning the Open Councils and for my MA thesis. Both of them have been very generous concerning time given to me; The Visiting Professor of Politics, Mr. Spring Poug, has offered many priceless suggestions for references. His main comments focused on the

The Open Councils

Open Council's compatibility with the needs of the modern Saudi people. He questioned me as to whether KSA is pressurised to employ a sort of parliamentary democracy.

The Professor of Anthropology, Laura Nader, has encouraged me to expand the idea of cultural relativity, which has a very important part in this book. Also, she suggested some references, and asked me to clarify some points that had been explained insufficiently.

But, for me, the best event was when His Royal Highness Prince Salman bin 'Abdul-'Aziz met me to discuss the Open Councils. This meeting, which was of great benefit, is presented in the sixth chapter.

2-4: Questionnaire

In order to carry out a comprehensive survey that polled the Open Councils' beneficiaries, I distributed a questionnaire consisting of twelve open questions and comments of those polled. (See Appendix No. 3). This questionnaire has been given to some persons attending the Prince Salman bin 'Abdul-'Aziz's Open Council at the Headquarters of Riyadh Governorate. Its findings will be analysed in Chapter Six.

2-5: Summary

References indicated in this chapter are valuable sources of information about the Open Council. In fact, this council is rooted deeply in Islamic tradition as well as the traditions of the Arab nations. Some people think this institution is nothing but a carnival, others defend it as a vital establishment. In my opinion, the most important question is: What are the advantages of the Open Councils for the Saudi people? This question has to be considered regardless of whether the institution be democratic or dictatorial.

I argue that the Open Councils perfectly suit the Saudi people's characters. The Open Council is considered an Islamic convention of rule suitable for tribal societies, to which the majority of KSA's population belongs. The Council is simply a gathering to discuss specific problems in order to solve them and it is actually part of the daily life agenda for every family, tribe, and government official, including governors of provinces, ministers and the highest leadership in KSA.

Chapter Three

The Kingdom of Saudi Arabia's Historical Background and Geography

3 - 1: Foreword
3 - 2: Geography of Saudi Arabia
3 - 3: The Administrative Provinces
3 - 4: Saudi Arabia's Historical Background
3 - 4 - 1: The First Saudi Kingdom
3 - 4 - 2: The Second Saudi State
3 - 4 - 3: The Modern Saudi State: KSA
3 - 4 - 3 - 1: The Nature of Saudi Arabia's Political Development
3 - 4 - 3 - 2: The Stages of the Political Development in Saudi Arabia
3 - 5: Summary

3-1: Foreword

Most historians agree that the history of Saudi Arabia's royal family and its domination in the Arabian Peninsula are not accidental. Nevertheless, this historic development is rooted in the Arabian Peninsula's past history. At present, the Saudi Arabian regime is a continuation of The First Saudi Kingdom 1157-1233 AH (1744-1818 AD), and the Second Saudi State 1238-1309 AH (1823-1891 AD)[30].

If the development of the Saudi Kingdom, under Islamic rule, has had prominence for some foreign peoples, it is due to the marvellous accomplishments of the Saudi royal family. They have successfully controlled the Arabian Peninsula, distributed its fortunes amongst the Saudis, spread Islam, and encouraged the citizens to be devoted to Islam while preserving the Arabian Peninsula's unity and security.

In this chapter, I will summarise KSA's historical and geographical background in addition to attempting a quick review of political development and decision-making inside the Saudi Arabian government. The first part of this chapter tackles Saudi Arabia's geographical locality: it being of strategic importance in the Middle East. The second part deals with the establishment of the Saudi Kingdom by King 'Abdul-'Aziz.

3-2: Geography of Saudi Arabia

KSA is located in the most remote area of Southwest Asia. As a result, it occupies a strategic location between the Arabian Gulf and the Red Sea. Saudi Arabia takes up about four fifths of the Arabian Peninsula. Its population is nearly 16,984,388 - most of who inhabit villages and major cities[31]. Most of the territory of Saudi Arabia consists of desert. The area of KSA is over 2 million km². It is bordered by Kuwait, Iraq and Jordan in the North, and Bahrain, Qatar, the Arabian Gulf, the United Arab Emirates in the East, and the Sultanate of Oman, the

---

[30] Al-Qabba, Abdullah. *The Foreign Policy of The Kingdom of Saudi Arabia* (Riyadh, Al-Farazdaq's Press, 1986 AD) p. 63.

[31] *The Encyclopedia of King 'Abdul –'Aziz: "The Saudi Kingdom in a Hundred Years"*, (Riyadh: Al - 'Obaikan Bookshop, 1419 A.H / 1999 A.D) p. 7.

Justice is the foundation of Governance

Republic of Yemen in the South and the Red Sea in the West.

3-3: The Administrative Provinces

According to the division decided upon in the Provinces' System 1412 AH (1992 AD), Saudi Arabia is divided into thirteen administrative provinces (i.e. emirates) (See Appendix No. 4); each of which has an administrative ruler (an emir or governor) (Fig. 1). Each province contains administrative districts, which are governed by governors and principals. They are

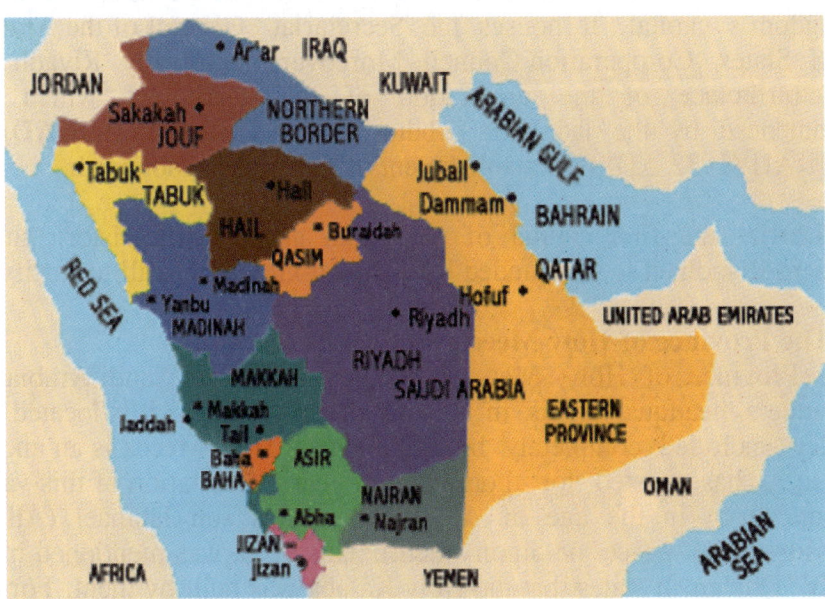

Fig.1 The Administrative Provinces of Saudi Arabia

supervised by the Emir of the Administrative Province. This system in its entirety is presided over by the Interior Minister who has direct contact with the King during cabinet sessions.

Briefly, Saudi Arabia's administrative provinces are:

1. The Province of Riyadh

The Riyadh province is the largest, most populated and most significant province of the Saudi Kingdom. It is situated in the middle of the country. A large portion of the Saudi population resides in this province, and so consequently it contains the largest number of

The Open Councils

administrative districts in comparison to other provinces. Its administrative districts are:

> Class A[32] administrative districts: Al-Dar'ia, Al-Kharj, Al-Doudami, Al-Mujamma'a, Al-Mir'ia, Al-Aflaj, Wadi Al-Dawasser, Al-Zalfi, Shaqra, as well as Houta Bani Tamim.
> Class B administrative districts: Afif, Al-Salil, Darma, Al-Muzahimya, Remah, Thadeq, Huraimila, Al-Hariq, and Al-Ghat.

The headquarters of this Emirate is situated in Riyadh, the Saudi Kingdom's capital. It houses the Secretariat General of the Arabian Gulf States Co-operation Council. Moreover, historically, Riyadh was the birthplace of the unification of the territories, which was commenced by the late King 'Abdul-'Aziz in 1319 AH (1902 AD). In 1351 AH (1932 AD) the establishment of KSA was announced.

Al-Dar'ia, the first capital of the Saudi state, is the historic site of ancient Riyadh; it is surrounded by a fifteen-kilometre wall to fortify it.

2. The Province of Holy Mecca

The Province of Holy Mecca is situated in Western Saudi Arabia. Its Emirate's headquarters is in the city of Holy Mecca. It is located in a valley encircled completely by mountains. Holy Mecca is an ancient town; it has existed for thousands of years. Habitation of this valley began first in the age of Abraham and his son Ishmael (Allah's blessings and peace be upon them). This event was mentioned in the Holy Qur'an. It states that the Holy Ka'aba was built by them. For this reason the Prophet Ishmael (Allah's Blessings and Peace be upon him) might have been the first man living in this area. Holy Mecca was built around the Holy Ka'aba. Consequently, her name has been derived from it. Holy Mecca's real history began in the epoch of Qussay bin Kilab bin Murra Al-Qurayshi who ruled Holy Mecca, in the middle of the fifth century AD. He established Dar Al-Nadwa as his headquarters. He also oversaw the reconstruction of Holy the Ka'aba upon firmer foundations.

Holy Mecca is the heart of the Islamic nation as it is the birthplace of Islam and a centre of civilisation. It embraces the Holy Places, which

---

[32] Districts are classed according to their land mass and demographic density.

The Open Councils

are beloved to all Muslims. Every year, millions of pilgrims visit, either on a minor pilgrimage or the major Hajj pilgrimage in response to Allah's command: {**And proclaim unto mankind the Pilgrimage. They will come unto thee on foot and on every lean camel; they will come from every deep ravine**} **Al-Hajj: 27**.

A merit of Holy Mecca is narrated by Al-Nassa'i, Al-Tirmadhi, as well as Ibn Majah that 'Adullah bin 'Udayy bin Al-Hamra who heard the Prophet Muhammad (PBUH) upon his camel in Mecca, say: " I swear by Allah, you are Allah's most beloved place in my heart. If I had not been forced to leave you, I would have not have done so". Another factor distinguishing Holy Mecca is its status as *qiblah*[33].

The province of Holy Mecca is comprised of the following administrative districts: Holy Mecca province contains three major cities: Holy Mecca (headquarters of the Emirate), Jeddah, and Al-Ta'if. It includes a large coastal region whose area is more than 500 km^2 and runs from Al-Qunfuza in the South to Rabegh in the North. It encompasses significant sections of the Hijaz mountains (i.e. Al-Ta'if).

3. The Province of Holy Medina

Holy Medina is situated to the North of the Holy Mecca province. The province of Tabouk in the North, the Qassim and Ha'il provinces in the East encircle it. This province envelops:

    Two administrative districts of Class A: Yanbu' and Al-'Ala,
    Four Class B administrative districts: Mahd Al-Zahab, Badr, Khaybar and Al-Hinkania).

The city of Holy Medina is the Emirate's headquarters. It is an important town, because it has a special place in Islam. It is the city of Prophet Muhammad (PBUH). He emigrated there from Mecca, in order to spread Islam and establish the Islamic State. He was warmly welcomed to the city and aided by its inhabitants. There He built the first mosque (Mosque of Qiba'). Holy Medina contains the Prophet Muhammad's Mosque, which is the second Holy Mosque that is visited by Muslims.

---

[33]'*Qiblah*' means 'the focus of attention' and the 'ideal'. Thus it also signifies the direction to which Muslims turn in praying all over the world: Mecca.

The Open Councils

It contains many prominent historic places related to Islam, including the tombs of the Prophet Muhammad (PBUH), three of the orthodox caliphs, and many of the Prophet's companions (may Allah be pleased with them). As a result, it is one of the greatest and most well known cities in the Islamic world.

Furthermore, Holy Medina has a significant Islamic establishment: King Fahd Publishers of the Holy Qur'an. It also includes the Islamic University at which students from around the Muslim world study Shari'a.

4. The Province of Qassim

In The Qassim Province, there are ancient valleys (e.g. the Wadi of Rimma, the longest valley in the Arabian Peninsula). Also, it is famous for its timeworn ruins, which show its ancient civilisation; in The Jawa' Springs the remains of Abla's[34] House are to be found. In Al-Assiah there is found Tamims' Nibaj known at the dawn of Islam. Buraida, a sizeable town, is the headquarters of the Qassim Emirate.

The Province of Qassim contains:
>Class A administrative districts: 'Unayza, Al-Ras, Al-Muzannab, and Al-Bakiria.
>Class B administrative districts: Al-Badai', Al-Assiah, Al-Nabhania, Al-Shamassia, 'Uyoun Al-Jawa and Riyadh Al-Khubara.

5. The Eastern Province

The Eastern Province lies in the Northeast of KSA on the Western coast of the Arabian Gulf. Al-Dammam is its headquarters. It includes varied governmental administrations. Al-Dammam City has witnessed great development and construction.

The Eastern province is subdivided into the following administrative districts:
>Class A administrative districts: Al-Ahsa, Hafr Al-Baten, Al-Jubail, Al-Qatif, as well as Al-Khubar.
>Class B administrative districts: Al-Khafji, Ras Tannoura, Buqaiq, Al-Na'iria, and Al-'Ulya.

---

[34] Abla was the beloved of the legendary hero of Arab folklore, Antar.

Economically, the Eastern province is regarded as the most important district of Saudi Arabia. Moreover, it plays a weighty role in the global economy for it contains about 25% of the world's oil reserves. Petroleum is the fountainhead of Saudi Arabia's economy; it is a strategic commodity, because it is the chief source of energy in the world. Following the discovery of the oil, cities have developed in the Eastern province. The largest one is Ras Tannoura, from which 90% of the Saudi Kingdom's oil and oil derivatives are exported. In Al-Zahran the A.R.A.M.CO headquarters and the campus of the King Fahd University for Petroleum and Minerals are situated.

6. The Province of 'Assir

The 'Assir province is situated in the Southwest portion of KSA. Historians and geographers concur that the name 'Assir originates from Al-'Usr (the difficulty) as its topography is difficult to traverse. Topographically, it consists of:

- The first portion 'Assir of Al-Surat, which is sub-classified into the Eastern fields region. From it, the river of Bisha flows. Crops are grown adjacent to its banks. The area of heights (Al-Surat or Al-Sarwat mountains ranges) is the heart of the region and has the highest population density. **A moderate summer** and agricultural steppes characterise it. It is where the Emirate's headquarters, Abha, is located.
- The Second Portion: Tuhama of 'Assir: It is subdivided into Al-Asdar's Tuhama, which lies between the mountain range and the coastal fields, containing many villages and farms. It is famous for beekeeping. In addition, it is distinguished by the cultivation of almonds, cacti, bananas and coffee. The other area is the coastal Tuhama, which are the coastal field of the Red Sea. Summer there is severely hot and humid, while it's winter is temperate. Beautiful shores, warm sands and highly fertile lands mark this region.

Administratively, the province of 'Assir is sub-partitioned into the following Administrative districts:

Class A administrative districts: Khamis, Mashit, Bisha, Al-Nammas and Muhail.

Class B administrative districts: 'Ubaida's Surat, Tathlith, Rijal of Alma', Belqarn, Uhud, Zahran Al-Janoub, and Al-Majarda.

7. The Province of Ha'il
The Ha'il province is in the Northwest of Saudi Arabia. It is ringed by the northern borders and Al Jaouf provinces, the provinces Tabuk and Holy Medina as well as the province of Qassim on the East. Ha'il City is the headquarters of the Emirate.

Additionally, there are:
Class A administrative districts: Buq'a.
Class B administrative districts: Al-Ghazala, and Al-Shannan.

The town of Ha'il lies 690 km from Saudi Arabia's capital. It is 915 metres above sea level. It is very well known for its moderate atmosphere and fresh water.

8. The Province of Tabouk
The Tabouk province is situated in the Northwest of the Saudi Kingdom, near the Holy Land of Palestine. It is encircled by the heights. It has been populated since ancient times. Located in or around it, are inhabitants of the Thicket and Prophet Shu'aib's homeland. In the 9th year AH (c. 630 AD), the Prophet Muhammad (PBUH) conquered it. Tabouk City is the headquarters of the Emirate. It is sub-divided into:

Class A administrative districts Al-Wajh, Diba' and Taima'.
Class B administrative districts Amlaj and Haql.

9. The Province of Al-Baha
Al-Baha province is in the westen centre of KSA; its borders touch the provinces of Holy Mecca and 'Assir. It is encircled by prominent cities, like Al-Ta'if to the North, Bisha to the East, Abha to the South, as well as the Red Sea and some parts of the Holy Mecca Province on the West. Although the province of Al-Baha is located in the desert region, its climate is temperate due to its altitude; winter is cool and summer is moderate. Al-Baha town is the headquarters of the Emirate. It is sub classified into the following provinces:

Class A administrative districts: Baljarshi, Al-Mandaq, and Al-Mukhwa.
Class B administrative districts: Al -'Aqiq, Qulwa and Al-Qari.

10. The Province of Northern Borders
This province is located in the North of KSA. The city of 'Ar'ar is the headquarters of this Emirate. It is sub-partitioned into:
>A Class A administrative district: Rafha'.
>A Class B administrative district: Tarif.

The Province has developed rapidly in all aspects of life. The Emirate's headquarters, 'Ar'ar; is a modern town populated by Bedouins who have settled there seeking to earn a living.

11. The Province of Al-Jaouf
Al Jaouf province is located among the Northern Provinces of KSA, for it is encircled by: the Province of Northern Borders, Tabouk Province, and the Province of Ha'il. Its topography is varied; the most crucial features are the depression of Doumat, Al-Jandal town and the city of Sikaka. The most substantial valley is Al-Sarhan Wadi that runs from Doumat Al-Jandal to the East of Jordan.

In addition to The Emirate's Headquarters (Sikaka Town), there are:
>A Class A administrative district: Al-Qariat.
>Class B administrative districts: Doumat Al-Jandal.

Historically, Doumat Al Jandal is one of the most prominent cities, which is famous for manufacturing swords, daggers, and guns.

12. The Province of Jazan
The Jazan Province is in the Southwest of Saudi Arabia. It is surrounded by Yemen's Borders to the South, the Province of 'Assir to the North, nearly 25 km of The Red Sea Coast on the West, and the province of 'Assir to the East. It is distinguished by diverse topography between the coastal plains to the heights. The climate allows for a hot summer and a moderate winter.

Administratively, it is sub-classified into the following districts:
>Class A administrative districts: Sabia', abu 'Arish and Sameta.
>Class B administrative districts: Al-Harth, Damad, Al-Rith, Bish, Fursan, Al Da'ir, Uhud Al-Masarha, Al-'Idabi, Al-'Arida, and Al Qias.

The city of Jazan is the Emirate's headquarters. The city has witnessed tremendous progress. It is very famous for fishing and trade.

13. The Province of Najran
The Najran Province is seen as a prominent district of Saudi Arabia because of its ancient history, highly strategic location and economic importance.

The Province of Najran is in the Southwest of the Saudi Kingdom. High mountains ring it, but to the East their altitudes decrease until they sink into the sands of the Empty Quarter. The city of Najran lies on flat lands, with the river Najran flowing through the centre towards the sands of the Empty Quarter. Its climate is somewhat continental.

Najran is the headquarters of the Emirate. It is sub-divided into:

    A Class A Administrative district: Sharoura.

    Class B Administrative districts: Hibbouna, Badr Al-Janoub, Ludmih, Khabbash and Thar

3 - 4: Saudi Arabia's Historical Background

3 - 4 - 1: The First Saudi Kingdom 1157 - 1233 AH (1744 -1891 AD)
On 1157 AH (1744 AD) Imam Muhammad bin Sa'ud established The First Saudi Kingdom. On that occasion Sheikh Muhammad bin 'Abdul-Wahhab was hospitably received in the city of Al-Dar'ia. The two leaders did their best to spread his particular Islamic doctrine, which became known as Wahhabism, across the entirety of the Arabian Peninsula. In 1179-1218AH (1765-1803 AD) 'Abdul-'Aziz bin Muhammad bin Sa'ud became Emir of Al-Dar'ia after his father's death. He continued his father's support of Sheikh Muhammad bin 'Abdul-Wahhab and his mission. 1218-1229 AH (1803-1814 AD), Sa'ud bin 'Abdul-'Aziz (known as Sa'ud the Great) was in power, maintaining his support of Sheikh bin 'Abdul-Wahhab's policies. The Ottoman Empire resisted him. After his father's death 'Abdullah bin Sa'ud came to power. He faced much resistance from the Ottoman State. As a result, he lost some territory including Mecca and Medina. Thereafter, in 1223 AH (1818 AD) the First Saudi Kingdom was destroyed by the Egyptian-Ottoman Army, when they had stormed its capital Al-Dar'ia.[35]

---

[35] Al Saud, Mashaal, *"Permanence and Change: An Analysis of The Islamic Political Culture of Saudi Arabia with Special Reference to The Royal Family"* (PhD Diss., Claremont Graduate School, 1982 A.D) p. 53.

3 - 4 - 2: The Second Saudi State 1238 -1309 AH (1823-1891 AD)

In 1238 AH (1823 AD), the Second Saudi State was established by Turki bin 'Abdullah bin Muhammad bin Sa'ud. He made Riyadh his capital in order to bring peace to the Najd area. His reign began after defeating the Egyptian-Ottoman army at Riyadh in 1240 AH. (1824 AD)

Because The First Saudi Kingdom had succeeded in spreading security and stability in the area, the Second Saudi State had strong foundations and good support. Consequently, most of the lands controlled by The First Saudi Kingdom were restored. The Second Saudi State continued the prosperous rule of the nation until it spread westward in 1309 AH (1891 AD).[36]

3 - 4 - 3: The Modern Saudi State: KSA

Nowadays, the Kingdom of Saudi Arabia is still largely as the late King 'Abdul-'Aziz Al Sa'ud unified the country under the rule of Shari'a; on 1351 AH (1932 AD) all the districts were unified to create Saudi Arabia. The modern Saudi Arabia has existed for some 70 years. Thus, King 'Abdul-'Aziz is the inventor of the present-day Saudi state, whose history commenced on 1319 AH (1902 AD).

King 'Abdul-'Aziz was born in 1293 AH / 1880 AD in Riyadh into a family well known for leadership.[37] He had grown up under the wing of his father, who commissioned 'Ulama to teach him Islam. For some 20 years, he lived with his family in Kuwait, the place of his exile. He became greatly concerned about his homeland Najd, insisting that one day he would re-establish control over the region.

In 1319 AD (1902 AD), he recaptured Riyadh by means of a quick offensive. Between 1319 and 1338 AH (1902 and 1921 AD), on the strength of series of military campaigns, King 'Abdul-'Aziz gained

---

[36] *The Encyclopedia of King 'Abdul - 'Aziz, op.cit.*, pp. 27-31.

[37] Al Sa'ud, Talal bin 'Abdul-'Aziz. *Images of King 'Abdul -'Aziz's life* (Riyadh: Al Fakhiria Publications and Al-Katib Al-Arabi Publication House, Beirut 1405 A.H / 1985 A.D, The Second Edition) p. 26.

power over Najd.[38] This was the commencement of the era of modern Saudi Arabia. King 'Abdul- 'Aziz Al Sa'ud spent more than thirty years unifying the Kingdom. On 21 Jumada Al-Awwal 1351 AH (23 September 1932 AD), the provinces of Najd, Al-Ahsa', 'Assir, and Al-Hijas were combined with Riyadh, allowing the establishment of Saudi Arabia (The Monarchical Decree Law No. 2716 17 Jumada Al-Awwal 1351 AH and Umm Al-Qura[39], Issue No. 406 22 Jumada Al-Awwal 1351 AH).

On 1364 AH (1945 AD), Saudi Arabia became a founding member of the United Nations Organisation. It became one of the original fifty members by subscribing to the Charter of the United Nations.

King 'Abdul-'Aziz - who died on the morning of Monday 2 Rabi' Al-Awwal 1373 AH (9 November 1953 AD) and whose body was transported to Riyadh and laid to rest in the Royal Family's graveyard - is regarded as a founder of the modern Saudi state.

King Sa'ud (1373-1384 AH / 1953-1964 AD). On 16 Muharram 1352 AH (11 May 1933 AD), the authorised representatives and Shura Councils was in session and ratified a decision to recognise Prince Sa'ud, The eldest son of King 'Abdul-'Aziz as Crown Prince in order to give him a hand in ruling. In his youth, he had acquired good diplomatic experience during his visits to neighbouring Arab states, as well as some other countries.[40]

In addition to the above mentioned, he made use of his practice of administration when his late father was uniting the country, and during the last days of King 'Abdul-'Aziz's Life.[41]

---

[38] Al Zarkali, Khair Al Din, *The Manual of Monarch 'Abdul –'Aziz's Biography* (Beirut: Dar El - Ilm Lilmalayin, Beirut 1991 A.D, The Seventh Edition) p. 315 & after.

[39] Umm Al-Qura is the Official Government Gazette - where all the official announcements and decrees can be found.

[40] Iqbal. Muhammad. op.cit., pp. 52 - 53.

[41] For further information, see: *The World Arab Encyclopedia, Volume No. 12* (The Establishment of Encyclopedia works for Publishing & Distribution, Riyadh) p. 26.

Justice is the foundation of Governance

For this reason, on 1373 AH (1953 AD), when Sa'ud was King after his father had died, it was the beginning of a new era for KSA, which became a modern society.

Indeed, most of the monarchical legislative decrees concerning administration that were issued by King Sa'ud are still the foundation of the modern governmental system of KSA. During his rule, the first ministries' buildings were put up in Saudi Arabia, hospitals as well as other civil institutions were established and the Hajj fees were cancelled.

In Muhammad Iqbal's book about Saudi Arabia, it was mentioned:

> "King Sa'ud shall be unforgettable, for real achievements have come into being: in the city of Riyadh the first modern university (King Sa'ud University) and the Islamic University of Holy Medina, have been set up. Moreover, at the same time a technical institute was established in order to enable technicians to be trained at all levels. In Riyadh, Holy Mecca, and Holy Medina, money was spent".[42]

The expansion of the Mosque of Holy Medina was initiated to ensure the comfort of pilgrims. This was ordered by late King 'Abdul-'Aziz before he passed away (may Allah have mercy on him).[43]

King Faisal (1384-1395 AH/1964-1975 AD). King Faisal's era marked the start of focusing more on internal and external affairs and enhancing the role of the Saudi Kingdom in the global arena. Certain significant events also took place in the 1960s.

One of King Faisal's most prominent contributions was visiting other Islamic countries to strengthen Islamic solidarity and back up Muslim minorities. He also gave strong support to the Palestinian cause; he supported the Palestinian Liberation Organisation and worked hard to solve the Palestinian question.

---

[42] Iqbal, *op. cit.* p.p. 53.

[43] *The Encyclopaedia of King 'Abdul Aziz*, op. cit. P. 66.

The Open Councils

King Faisal played an effective role in the Arab - Israeli Conflict in 1393 A.H /1973, when he discontinued exporting crude oil to the Western world so affecting the West's position. In addition he stood powerfully against Communism, warning of its spread in the Arab and Islamic worlds.

Between (1390 A.H / 1970 A.D TO 1395 A.H / 1975 A.D), King Faisal showed his foresight in economic planning when the first Five Year Development Plan was adopted in KSA. In addition to the economy, the late King was also engaged in Industry, and agriculture. Some agricultural projects included irrigation, drawing off water, Al-Rimal (in Al-Ihsa'), Hardh, Abha etc. There was more exploration to find minerals and the Petromin Establishment was formed.

Under his governance the education system was developed - especially the education of women. His efforts also included improving social conditions, such as: insurance, taking care of the young, and social security. He was interested in the development of transportation and telecommunication[44] during his reign and did much to further agriculture. Grain warehouses and mills were built. He also encouraged industry, ordering the establishment of the Ministry of Industry and Electricity[45]

King Khalid (1395-1402 A.H/ 1975-1982 A.D). During King Khalid's rule, Saudi Arabia continued to develop. He applied various developmental programs. After the second Five-Year Development Plan had been accomplished successfully, the third Five-Year Development Plan was initiated. It aimed at finalising comprehensive development in Saudi Arabia. As a result, the Saudi Kingdom witnessed immense progress in all areas of life. Consequently, inside the country, the standard of living rose dramatically. The Kingdom of Saudi Arabia became respected politically and economically.[46]

Custodian of the two Holy Mosques, King Fahd (1402 AH / 1982 AD). If history records the truth, King Fahd will be remembered as playing a prominent part in building the modern Saudi State.

---

[44] *ibid.*, p.p. 72 – 73.

[45] *Ibid.*, p.p. 78 – 79.

[46] For More Information see: the *World Arab Encyclopedia*, Volume No. 10. p. 10.

When King Fahd came into power, he had already obtained a great deal of experience and a true faith, acquired by bearing heavy responsibilities upon his shoulders. He developed his trustworthiness and deep faith during the time of his late father King 'Abdul-'Aziz, then in the rule of the late Kings' Sa'ud, Faisal and Khalid. During that time he had been in numerous sensitive appointments. In each, he had been outstandingly successful. In this way he became a very experienced leader.

King Fahd had taken up the mission of expanding the two Holy Mosques. He made history when he became the first Islamic leader to be named "The Custodian of the two Holy Mosques" replacing "His Royal Highness". At present, he still continues his efforts at modernising the Kingdom. Under his reign, Saudi Arabia completed many unique achievements during the 20th century.[47]

Some of the most significant historical achievements of the Custodian of the two Holy Mosques, King Fahd bin 'Abdul –'Aziz, are as follows:

1 - On 1410 A.H. / 1990 AD, when Kuwait had been invaded by the Iraqi president, Saddam Hussein, King Fahd embraced Kuwaiti leaders and citizens, and welcomed them into the country. He also undertook the responsibility of calling Islamic, Arabic and friendly forces to be posted inside his homeland near the Kuwaiti borders with the aim of liberating Kuwait.

2 - The project of the Custodian of the two Holy Mosques was to expand the two Holy Mosques and their surrounding plazas in Mecca and Medina, as the number of Muslims arriving for pilgrimage increased. In addition, King Fahd kept developing the Holy Mosques with the latest air-conditioning and lighting equipment. He also insisted on the continuing maintenance of the Holy Places day and night, thereby making a successful Islamic investment and one of his historic achievements. The interest in the Holy Places - Mecca and Medina - shown by King Fahd - may Allah bless him - has a great impact upon Muslims who were impressed by the comfort, safety, security and peace during the rites of *al-Hajj*.

---

[47] Rashid, Nasser and Esber, Shaheen. *op.cit.*, p.65.

3 - King Fahd established a complex for printing and publishing the Holy Qur'an. This publishing complex aims to protect the Holy Qur'an from the serious mistakes committed by some publishing houses, as well as fulfilling the needs of the Islamic world for copies of Holy Qur'an and its different translations.

4 - In 1412 H / 1992 AD King Fahd, the Custodian of the Two Holy Mosques, established the basic system of ruling to develop the political system in Saudi Arabia. In 1414 H /1994 AD, he implemented the provincial Shura Councils and Cabinet forms of government. They were a big step forward in building the establishments of the State (see appendixes: 2-5).

3 - 4 - 3 - 1: The nature of Saudi Arabia's political development.

When the majority of the Arabian Peninsula had been unified by King 'Abdul-'Aziz, in a general meeting, most of the tribes' sheikhs and consultants agreed upon calling the new state: "The Kingdom of Saudi Arabia." Then, King 'Abdul-'Aziz directly ruled the country, aided by Princes appointed by him in the Kingdom's various regions. Those Emirs had been prepared by King 'Abdul-'Aziz in order to suit the circumstances of each province. Each Prince was looked on as His Royal Highness' representative in each district. The King himself administered military affairs as well as foreign policy.[48]

Advisors of the King used to consult and back him up in everything. Later on, they became the Royal Diwan Members. To them, it was obvious that the King depended on the Holy Qur'an as well as the Sunnah as the basis of his rule. In addition to the above mentioned, he sought the advice of the 'Ulama.

In 1345 AH / 1925 AD, in Holy Mecca, the Shura Council was created by him to develop autonomy for the nation. This was the next step after the invention of the Domestic Council. Consequently, the Kingdom was put on the right path towards successful administration. The Cabinet was formed, which carried out the majority of executive functions in looking after the country (see Figures: 2, 3).[49]

---

[48] Al - Jahni, Ed. *The Council of Ministers in Saudi Arabia* (Riyadh, Al - Majed Press, 1984 A.D) pp. 60 – 61.

[49] Dahlan, Ahmad. *op.cit.*, p. 125.

The Open Councils

We should realise the role played by the Saudi leadership in this progress. In Summer Scott Huyette's Book "Political Adaptation in Saudi Arabia", it is noted that "founding the Saudi Kingdom's Cabinet has been a response to the needs of the time".[50] The Cabinet's energy represents the dynamic nature and openness of Saudi rule. "Because of the fundamental role played by the Ministers' Council in attempting to modernise the country", the author later asserts, "it has become a centre for political power and decision making in the Kingdom of Saudi Arabia".[51]

Saudi Arabia's leadership gave power to a political council consisting of leaders from various districts called the cabinet. It has enforceable power in Saudi political decisions.

The King makes executive and legislative decisions. Sometimes this includes judicial authority. He also has the duty of accepting the credentials of all foreign diplomats and appointing ambassadors to foreign countries, He appoints all of the top civil and military officials, and signs all laws. In addition, he is the highest appellate authority, and is the only official to have the power of clemency.[52]

Figure (3) shows us the socio-political structure that enables the Open Council as well as the Cabinet to satisfy the needs of the citizens, provide an appropriate official response to their problems and obtain their support.

---

[50] Scott Huyette, Summer. *Political Adaptation in Saudi Arabia: A study of the Council of Ministers* (Boulder, Colo., Westview, 1985 A.D) p. 80.

[51] *Ibid.*, p.p. 80 - 81).

[52] Al-Saud, Mashaal, *op. cit.*, p.p. 103 - 104.

The Open Councils

Justice is the foundation of Governance

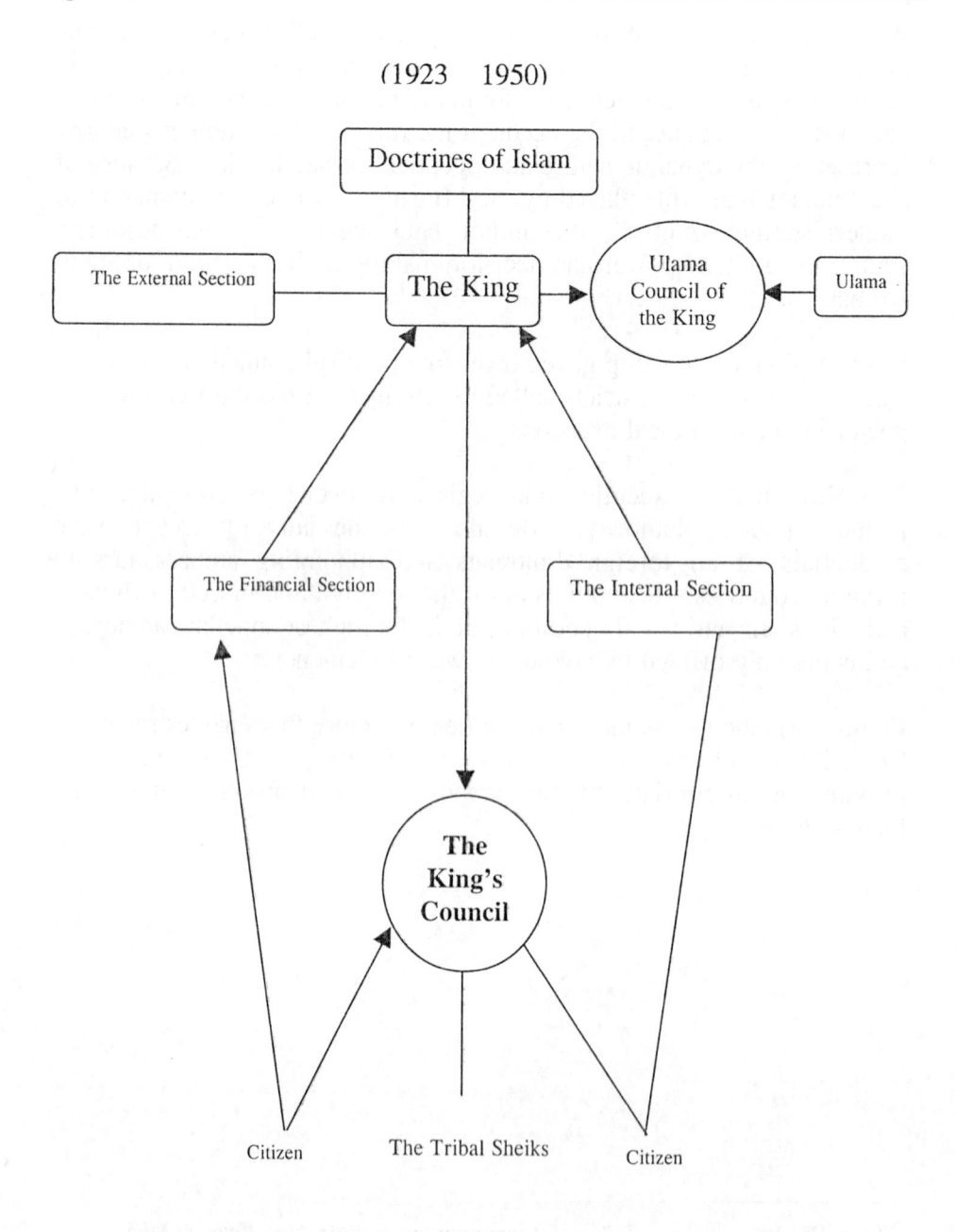

(1923   1950)

```
                    Doctrines of Islam
                            |
                            v
  The External Section → The King → Ulama Council of the King ← Ulama
                            
         The Financial Section      The Internal Section
                    ↘        ↓        ↙
                     The King's Council
                    ↗        |        ↖
              Citizen   The Tribal Sheiks   Citizen
```

Figure (2): The Political System during King 'Abdul –'Aziz's Era

The Open Councils

Justice is the foundation of Governance

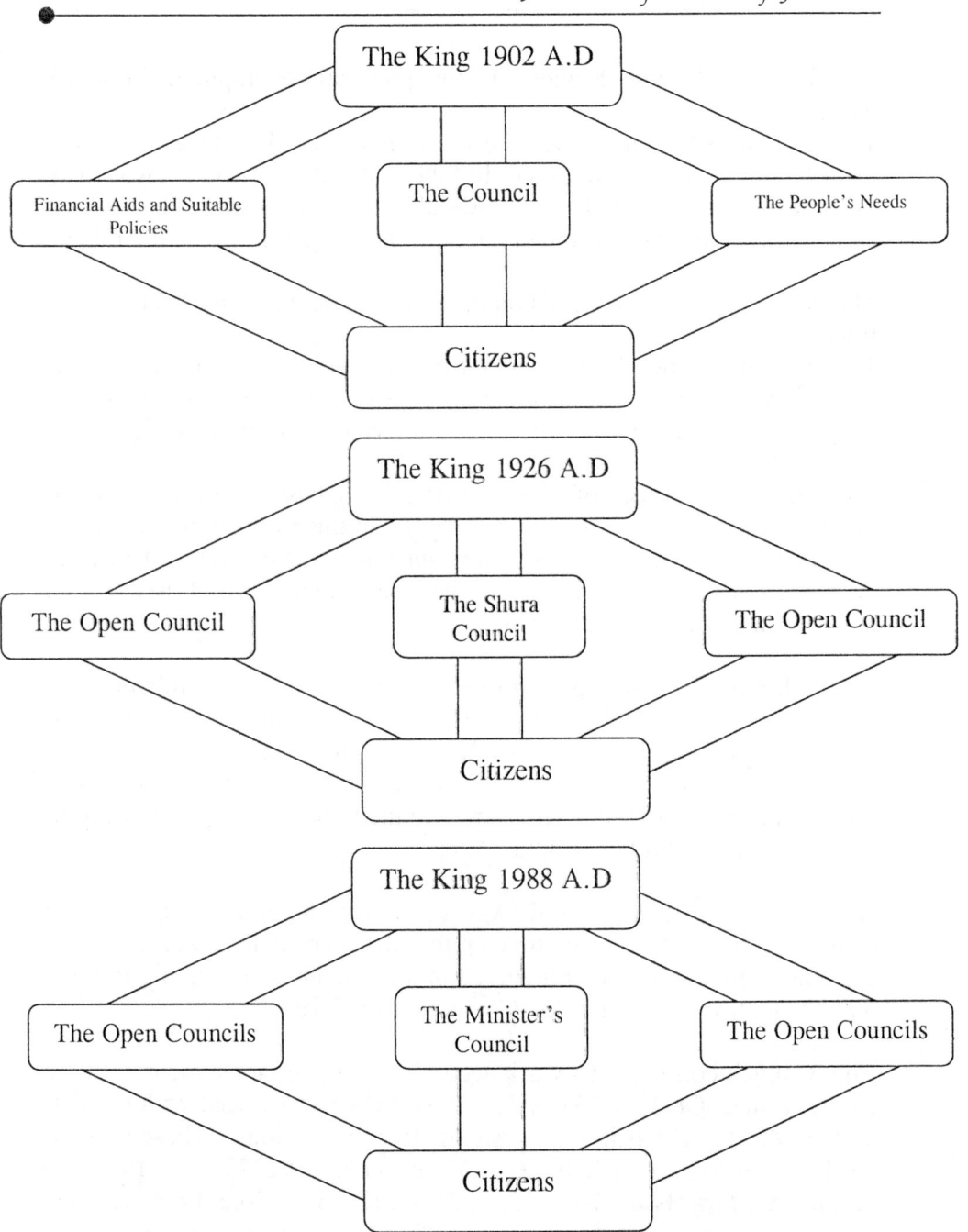

```
                    ┌──────────────────┐
                    │ The King 1902 A.D│
                    └──────────────────┘
         ┌──────────────┐  ┌──────────────┐  ┌──────────────┐
         │Financial Aids│  │ The Council  │  │The People's  │
         │and Suitable  │  │              │  │   Needs      │
         │  Policies    │  │              │  │              │
         └──────────────┘  └──────────────┘  └──────────────┘
                         ┌──────────────┐
                         │   Citizens   │
                         └──────────────┘

                    ┌──────────────────┐
                    │ The King 1926 A.D│
                    └──────────────────┘
   ┌─────────────────┐  ┌──────────────┐  ┌─────────────────┐
   │ The Open Council│  │  The Shura   │  │ The Open Council│
   │                 │  │   Council    │  │                 │
   └─────────────────┘  └──────────────┘  └─────────────────┘
                         ┌──────────────┐
                         │   Citizens   │
                         └──────────────┘

                    ┌──────────────────┐
                    │ The King 1988 A.D│
                    └──────────────────┘
   ┌──────────────────┐ ┌──────────────┐ ┌──────────────────┐
   │ The Open Councils│ │The Minister's│ │ The Open Councils│
   │                  │ │   Council    │ │                  │
   └──────────────────┘ └──────────────┘ └──────────────────┘
                         ┌──────────────┐
                         │   Citizens   │
                         └──────────────┘
```

Figure (3): Development of the practical & political measures for the Open Councils of the Saudi Kingdom.

The Open Councils

3 - 4 - 3 - 2: The Stages of the political development in Saudi Arabia.

The systems of ruling, the Shura Council, the Provinces, and the Ministers Council, established by the Custodian of the Two Holy Mosques, King Fahd bin 'Abdul-'Aziz, are ways by which modernisation has been brought about in the Kingdom of Saudi Arabia.

The system of rule depends on brotherhood between the ruler and the ruled.
The system of the Shura Council relies only on Islam. The district system is created to go side by side with the latest developments occurring in Saudi Arabia. The four systems are derived from Shari'a.

The different missions of the Government emphasise the importance of the task of ensuring that the country's administration concentrates on the welfare of all citizens, as well as inhabitants inside KSA. The stage of modernisation we witness confirms the significance of establishing new systems in this phase of progress.

1.   Birth and Development of the Council of Saudi Ministers:
On Zull Al Hijja 1372 AH / July 1953 AD, the first Council of Ministers was formed, headed by King 'Abdul-'Aziz. After that, at the beginning of Safar 1373 AH / October 1953 AD, King 'Abdul-'Aziz issued an act creating the Ministers' Council under the chairmanship of Crown Prince Sa'ud bin 'Abdul-'Aziz.

After a month, King 'Abdul-'Aziz died. King Sa'ud bin 'Abdul-'Aziz came to power and decided to keep the Ministers as they were. Due to the many issues and tasks involved in the change of leadership fixing a date for the first session of the Council was delayed.[53]

The Council continued its work according to the establishment's decree for a while. On 12/7/1373 AH / 1954 AD, it was issued with the first system of the Council and systems for its sections. These systems worked for four and a half years. Then, on 22/10/1378 AH / 1958 AD (Umm Al-Qura Issue No. 1508, 21/7/1373 AH / 26/3/1954 AD. and

---

[53] Al-Baz, Ahmad. "Development of The Political and Administrative System inside Saudi Arabia", Riyadh, Al-Shibl Publishing House, 1417 A.H, pp. 182-183.

The Open Councils

Umm Al-Qura Issue No. 1717, 27/10/1377 AH / 16/5/1958 AD), a modified system for the Council was issued. This was in operation for more than thirty-six years, with some changes from time to time. On 3/3/1414 AH / 21/8/93AD, a new system for the Council was implemented. (The Royal Act No. (A / 13), Dt. 3/3/1414 A.H)

Founding the Council is regarded as an important stage in developing the administration as well as policies of the Kingdom of Saudi Arabia. It was designed to create a comprehensive organisational structure to cover the whole nation. To this end, the Viceroy of Hijaz, its cadres, and *Al-Wakala* Council (the administrative council), were cancelled.

2. Rotation of the members of the Ministers' Council:

The leaders of the Saudi Kingdom realised the importance of having new Ministerial blood. For this reason, on 3/3/1414 AH, the Monarchical Act No. A/17 was issued, limiting the Council of Ministers' period to four years. After this period, it was to be re-formed. If the period was over before the re-formation, the Council's work should proceed until the issue of a Monarchic Decree.

This system has enabled many highly qualified Saudis to serve the homeland through the Council of Ministers. Thus we can see how the Kingdom of Saudi Arabia has developed as a politically united sovereign entity, and hopefully, with the guidance of Allah, will continue to do so.

Saudi Arabia's political and administrative system is still progressing, along with the development of its human society. As has been mentioned, it was small as well as simple, then it grew according to the situations surrounding Saudi Arabia and in keeping with Shari'a.[54]

3 - 5: Summary

This chapter has focussed on geography and the politico-historic development of the Saudi Kingdom. It is located in a very prominent geographic place. It has deep-rooted traditions and strong leadership. The Cabinet system does its best to fulfil the people's needs.

---

[54] Al-Baz, Ahmad. *Ibid.*, p.p. 253 – 254.

Chapter Four

The Religious and Cultural Basis of the Islamic State

4 - 1: Foreword
4 - 2: The Islamic Political Regime's Structure
4 - 3: The Authorities of Islamic State
4 - 4: The Kingdom of Saudi Arabia's Ruling System
4 - 4 - 1: The Limits of the King's Authority
4 - 5: The Tribal Model of the Arabian Peninsula
4 - 6: Summary

4 - 1: Foreword

In this chapter, the author shows how the doctrines of Islam and conventions of culture have shaped rule in Saudi Arabia. Saudi Arabia's tribal traditions are discussed, as well as the manner in which the tribes are linked.

4 - 2: The Islamic Political Regime's Structure

The three fundamental principles upon which the Islamic political system relies - monotheism, the messages of Islam, and the Caliphate - need to be understood more fully in order to comprehend the political system.[55]

4 - 2 - 1: Monotheism

'Abdul-Karim Zaidan writes of monotheism in Islam, "it is the fundamental belief that there is only one God, Allah, the Lord of the Universe...and every resolution turns around Monotheism".[56]

This belief is that there is no God except Allah, the Creator, the Provider and the absolute Master of this universe and all that exists. He is the only Legislator who has absolute command, and he is the only One who merits all worship and obedience. Allah has passed to human beings all that exists in this Universe to use in accordance with His guidance. Therefore, no human being has the right to decide what the purpose of life is, nor to implement his own moral code. This can only be an absolute right of Allah who created human beings and endowed them with mental and physical capabilities.

The concept of Islamic governorship does not grant power to human beings to change a law revealed by Allah. He is the Absolute Master and His commands form the Islamic code, which has to be implemented in all aspect of human life including governance.

---

[55] Al-Moudawi, Abu-Al-'Aala. *The Way of Islamic Life* (Riyadh: Press of The General Administration's Chairmanship for: Islam's Studies, Giving Formal Legal Opinions, Missionary Activity, and Guidance, 1984 A.D) pp. 36 – 37.

[56] Zaidan, 'Abdul-Karim. *The Fundamentals of the Call to Islam* (Beirut, Baghdad, Al-Rissala Establishment, Al-Quds Library, Second Edition, 1407 A.H) p. 24.

"Monotheism is the core of Islam and its foundation. All rules, commands, procedures, emanate from Monotheism, which strike roots in the hearts of believers".[57]

4 - 2 - 2: The Message
It is through the Message that man received the Shari'a. There are two sources for Shari'a:
- The Holy Book of Islam (the Qur'an), in which Allah set forth His creed and Shari'a.
- The Prophetic Sunnah.

The general doctrine for rule amongst Muslims is mentioned in the Holy Qur'an. More detailed interpretations of these are given in the Prophetic Sunnah to provide a full model of life.

4 - 2 - 3: Caliphate
Caliphate means 'representation' or 'trusteeship'. According to the Islamic religion, man is the Caliph on Earth. Because of the characteristics and capabilities given to man by Allah, divine authority has to be implemented in this world. Also, man is to be responsible and authoritative within the framework of Islam. As a result, in Islam, government is responsible for protecting religion and worldly policies. The state is the human Caliphate under the power of Allah the Almighty.

The Holy Qur'an decides that the goal of ruling is justice as well as the spread of moral values. For example, in the Surah An-Nisa', Verse no. 58, the Almighty Lord says: { **Allah doth command you...if ye judge between people, that ye judge justly** }. This means that the Islamic religion deals with all citizens within an ethical system. Consequently, the Islamic State has the power of developing programs for the welfare of humanity.

Islamic religion imposes a state obligation to look after moral values in all aspects of life. In this way, the political principles formed are out of respect for this. The Islamic State refuses, in all circumstances, deception and cruelty, both nationally and internationally. The priorities are only truth, faithfulness, and fairness

---

[57] Zaidan, 'Abdul-Karim. *op. cit.*, p. 24.

4 – 3 The Authorities of the Islamic State

Both political scientists and various political regimes have agreed that states must possess the following distinct types of authority: legislative, judicial, and executive. However, in Islamic states such as the Kingdom of Saudi Arabia, the legislative authority is interpreted differently. The legislative fundamentals have relied, for more than fourteen centuries, on the Holy Qur'an which was revealed to Our Prophet Muhammad (PBUH).

As a result, Saudi Arabia has employed Shura as an organising power, in addition to the Council of Ministers, as an executive and legislative authority. The Council is completely free to utilise Shari'a in all aspects of Saudi life.

In the Islamic State, legislation is restricted to Shari'a and the Legislator (the Almighty Allah) in making laws. Moreover, any legislative institution must not adjust a Qur'anic statement or true Hadith. However, concerning ambiguous doctrines, as well as more recent antecedents, the Council of Open 'Ulama has to define the Shari'a's judgements. Thus, legislative authority in any Islamic state is, first and foremost, organisational in order, not totalitarian.

In the Islamic religion, judicial authority also depends on the Holy Qur'an and the Sunnah. In spite of the fact that the Prime Minister appoints judges, they are to be aware of their responsibilities in front of Allah. As a result, rulers and people are equal under the law.[58]

4 - 4: The Kingdom of Saudi Arabia's Ruling System

In the rule of Islam there is no clear separation between the religion and the State, because Islam organises all aspects of social and personal interaction by strictly following the religious doctrines mentioned in the Holy Qur'an, as well as the Holy Sunnah.

The Government of Saudi Arabia obeys the principles of Islamic Rule. Although the Lord is the Only Absolute Authority, the King represents it. Ibn Taymiyyah (may Allah have mercy on him) says, "the people's tutelage is, surely, a very prominent duty of religion. Almighty Allah has ordered us to

---
[58] Al Moudawi, Abu Al-'Aala. *op. cit.*, p. 37.

instruct in a friendly manner and forbid abomination. This is accomplished only through power, leadership, and obeying Allah. Punishment is employed by force."[59].

When a King comes to power, his citizens have to pay homage to him. This was an old tradition adopted by Muslim rulers. In the case of the Saudi Kingdom, homage is also made to the Crown Prince during the King's life, in order to avoid any conflict-taking place on the King's death. Paying homage is a solemn promise to obey what the Lord has sent down through His Messenger (PBUH). Paying homage also includes people of experience (mostly, at the present moment, 'Ulama and Chiefs of Justice).

4 - 4 - 1: Limits of the King's Authority

According to Islamic conventions, the Head of State has to consult faithful advisers to help him make decisions. In addition to his confidential consultants, the King meets the citizens, twice a week, in an Open Council. During this time they can be helped to solve their problems. He also meets a group of 'Ulama once a week. In many cases, the 'Ulama are significant censors of his authority. Verdicts of Islamic courts are applied respectfully even if they contradict the personal interests of the ruler, even if he has appointed the judges.

For example, a woman complained to the late King Faisal that a fence around a property of his had crossed into her land. She insisted that this had occurred because he was the King. He asked her to hand the case over to the Court. The Court's sentence was against the King and she obtained her rights from him.

In this way, the authority of the King can provide a means of justice. He is fully responsible before the Almighty. In the Islamic ideal, the King is confined within the Shari'a, and is not totalitarian.

4 - 5: The Tribal Model of the Arabian Peninsula

In the Arabian Peninsula, the tribe was the strongest social unit in the pre-Islamic Era. Throughout the ages, the tribe has been regarded as a major factor in the history of the Arabs. Members of these tribes are called "Bedouins".

---

[59] *"The Sultan is the Allah's Shade on The Earth"* from: Ibn Taymiyyah, Taqi Al Din Ahmad bin Abdul-Halim. *Legal Policy* (Riyadh: The General Presidency Of Ordering With Kindness And The Forbidding Of Wrong, 1412 AH/1992 AD) p.116.

The Open Councils

In the pre-Islamic Era, most tribes of the Arabian Peninsula waged wars against each other. They aimed at controlling as much land as they could in order to guarantee enough food as well as water for their animals.

After Islam had come into existence, this type of conflict died away. Through spreading Islam among the tribes, conflict was replaced by friendly relationships and co-operation. But, despite these fruits, sometimes conflicts did erupt, especially among the stronger tribes. Consequently, their was unrest in the Arabian Peninsula when the late King 'Abdul-'Aziz came to power. He put an end to these wars by unifying the tribes into one entity - the Kingdom of Saudi Arabia. As a result, in 1330 AH (1912 AD), the project of settling the tribes in Al-Badia was initiated. Islamic doctrines became more deeply rooted in the hearts of Saudi Arabia's people.

The tribal structure plays an important part in the self-regulation of the people, particularly in socio-economic matters. The tribal leaders also contribute to central government working under its supervision.[60]
In Saudi Arabia, the tribal model of rule has become an effective method of preserving stability and engaging tribes and tribal leaders in Shari'a-driven development. Monarchical rule in the country has systemised the tribal system and has transformed the state of conflict in tribal relations to one of peace.

4 - 6: Summary

In this chapter, we saw how religious principles as well as the Bedouin traditions have shaped the Kingdom of Saudi Arabia. These two basic factors remain elements that drive its current policies. The writer assumes that acknowledgement of these historic elements allow us to better understand the current Saudi form of government.

In the past, tribes had to live in a state of primitive 'Bedouinism' and continuous war. Later on, when the late King 'Abdul-'Aziz had united them, they accepted rule, encouraged by Islam. After that, tribal leaders became an efficient agent of Saudi Arabia's new regeneration, preserving local traditions in the hearts of the people. According to the author, understanding the system of Open Councils was a fundamental factor in achieving this progress, preserving the equilibrium between the unchangeable and the changeable. The Open Councils facilitate active contact enabling leaders to understand their citizens' needs.

---

[60] Al-Seflam, Ali. M. *"The Essence of Tribal Leaders Participation, Responsibilities, and Decisions in Some Local Government Activities in Saudi Arabia"* (Ph.D. Diss., Claremont Graduate School, 1982)

Chapter Five

International Comparisons

5 - 1: Foreword
5 - 2: Comparative Hypothesis
5 - 3: A View of the Relationship between the Type of Rule and the Saudi Style of Life
5 - 4: Analytical Comparisons
5 - 5: Summary

5 - 1: Foreword

Before we compare the Kingdom of Saudi Arabia's political systems and those of some Western countries, we will define the hypotheses of comparisons.

5 - 2: Comparative Hypothesis

5 - 2 - 1: The first hypothesis is called the hypothesis of historico-cultural comprehensiveness. This states that in order to understand how and why a human society has adopted its own political system, we have to acknowledge its history and the cultural models of its religion, family structures, education and economy. For example, if we wish to understand the USA's present political system, it is important to know the political genesis of the USA, and the history of the separation between the church and the state. The same concept applies to Saudi Arabia. It is not difficult for us to understand that the development of these two countries has been shaped by different structural and intellectual models. Consequently, there is a significant variation between their current systems of government. Such analysis can help in understanding that what is good for Western governments may not be acceptable in Oriental governments, and vice versa. We should evaluate the US system of rule by looking at US cultural traditions. Similarly, we will only reach an understanding of the ruling system of Saudi Arabia by examining it within its cultural context.

The historic dimensions of the modern US political system go back to Europe. European nations led explorations to the 'New World' (i.e. the Americas) and the British colonised North America's Eastern coast. European political development witnessed three broad stages: Theocratic monarchy, national rule (the emergence of dictatorships), and liberal democracy. In the Kingdom of Saudi Arabia, the political system is defined by Islam. Shari'a makes the ruler and the ruled equal, and is applied by the King. This monarchical system can be considered a natural progression of Islamic rule, which has developed through the stages of Prophethood, the Caliphate, the Umayyads and the glorious Abbasids.

5 - 2 - 2: The second hypothesis is related to social engineering. Before a system or tradition can be taken from one society to another, it is essential to study the chronicle and nature of the society that imports this system. For example, the Islamic political system of the Saudi Kingdom is at odds with modern US's history and conventions. Similarly, Western democracy does not suit the chronicle, culture, traditions and aspirations of the Kingdom of Saudi Arabia. Western governments have tried to export culture as well as technologies, regardless of the nature of this society, and the acceptance of intellectuals.

5 - 2 - 3: The third hypothesis: There is a danger for Western scholars in the comparative study of Oriental political and cultural systems that comparison and evaluation may be confused. Objectivity cannot be relied upon. Laura Nader and Edward Said have pointed out the problem of subjectivity in comparisons between the Orient and the Occident.

5 - 2 - 4: The fourth hypothesis: The union between religion and the ruling system in Saudi Arabia needs more detailed clarification. The interests of policy determine the political functions of governments in the West as secular regimes. These interests are not affected by religious doctrines, except through political lobbies. It is forbidden, culturally, in the West for the functions of the system of government to be defined directly by the Church, because of the separation of the Church and the State. For example, it is not possible for a clergyman, who is a member in the local City Council, to use his work to further his position as a cleric.

In Saudi Arabia, policies are determined differently. Roles and functions are directly determined according to religious principles. All governmental roles rely on specific criteria laid down by Shari'a. In the system of the Saudi Kingdom, religious functions are political. Both religious and political functions are the same. As result, the ruling system and the religion form one institution. The mission of the Saudi system of governmental includes a dimension of ethical responsibility which is absent in the principles of government in the West. It is a concept of Islam that all Muslims are brothers. This means that leaders are to be responsible for their citizens as members of one united family. Consequently, in the Kingdom of Saudi Arabia's government system political leaders and wealthy people are responsible before Almighty Allah and society. The King's Western counterpart may or may not believe that there is a religious significance to his job in the government. He does not assume that there is a religious commitment in his service to the public. In Saudi Arabia, all of the officials are committed morally to their people.

5 - 3: A View of the Relationship between the Type of Rule and the Saudi Style of Life

In any country, there will be supporters of the government, people opposing it, and the uncommitted. We can also find different groups of ethnic minorities. Figure (4) shows the writer's viewpoint concerning the comparative characteristics of two ruling systems. Is one regime better than another? Is Western democracy better than a just monarchy?

The educated reader will question the significance of the particular name of the regime, be it democracy or monarchy, but would judge the regime according to how the government suited the population governed. I think that the most important thing is the issue of principles employed by the system of government, its practices, and the benefits achieved for its citizens. The principles of Saudi Arabia declare that all persons are equal before the Shari'a. The task of Government is to satisfy its people. If the regime achieves its citizens' aspirations, its name is unimportant.

Societal Model	The Ruling System	The Way of Life
The Western model	Western democracy	'personal freedoms are secured by subjective laws.
The Saudi model	Islamic Monarchy	'personal freedoms are guaranteed by Shari'a.

Figure (4): A comparison between the features of the West's system of government and characteristics of the Kingdom of Saudi Arabia's ruling system.

The key to democracy lies in the recognition of choice. The U.S government provides for the things that the American population want. However, it is well known that the wishes of the individual may not coincide with the welfare of the public and state as a whole. Saudi Arabia's government also works towards achieving the aspirations of the Saudi people. The American people chose Western democracy. The

Saudi citizens prefer their model.

Each of these models has its advantages and disadvantages. Islam, adopted by the Saudi Kingdom rejects that which is *haram* (forbidden in Islam) and human jurisprudence accepts this judgement. As the Orient learns from the Occident, I hope that the Occident makes use of the successes of the Orient in the fields of both governance and lifestyle.

Another question that needs to be asked, however, is what happens when the economic system fails to achieve the material standard of living aspired to by the people? A defining factor is the relationship between resources and population. Government is successful when it responds quickly. This ability to react quickly is related to the capability of acquiring the right information from the decision-makers and the accessibility of the officials to the general public. The Open Council system does provide these two forms of communication. For example, in 1408 AH / 1988 AD when the Government had looked at how taxes paid by Saudis might clear the budget deficit, it came to a decision. However, within the Open Councils, the close ties between the ruler and the ruled who objected to this made the officials change their minds.

Finally, we will discuss a point in the Kingdom of Saudi Arabia's system of government compared with government systems in other Islamic countries. The Monarchy of Saudi Arabia is restricted in the procedures employed by it, as its constitution is the Holy Qur'an. For this reason, it is impossible to legislate according to individual desires. In other countries, it is possible to modify subjective constitutions for personal ends. To ensure correct procedures the King consults weekly with a council of 'Ulama about all matters. The relationship between the 'Ulama and the King is advisory, and he cannot argue with their pronouncements, which are derived from Shari'a. Thus it can be said that Saudi Arabia has a non-dictatorial Monarchical system compared with other regimes around the World. Figure (5) shows the restrictions that are imposed on the Monarchical system of the Saudi Kingdom.

The success of Saudi Arabia's system of government is, in general, Islam's success. In order to make the Islamic model of government in Saudi Arabia shine globally, we have to work hard in practising the doctrines of Islam. "We have to develop human society and nurture the country. Saudi Arabia's family is predestined to do so. This is its real challenge".[61]

---

[61] Al - Faisal, Khalid. *op. cit.*, P.P. 37 – 38.
―― *The Open Councils*

Justice is the foundation of Governance

Figure (5): Restrictions on the Saudi Monarchy

Other monarchies are able to go beyond the limits of the general order i.e. the subjective constitution

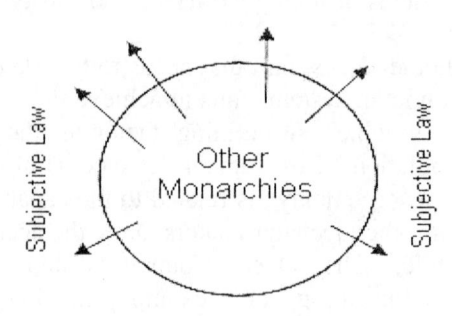

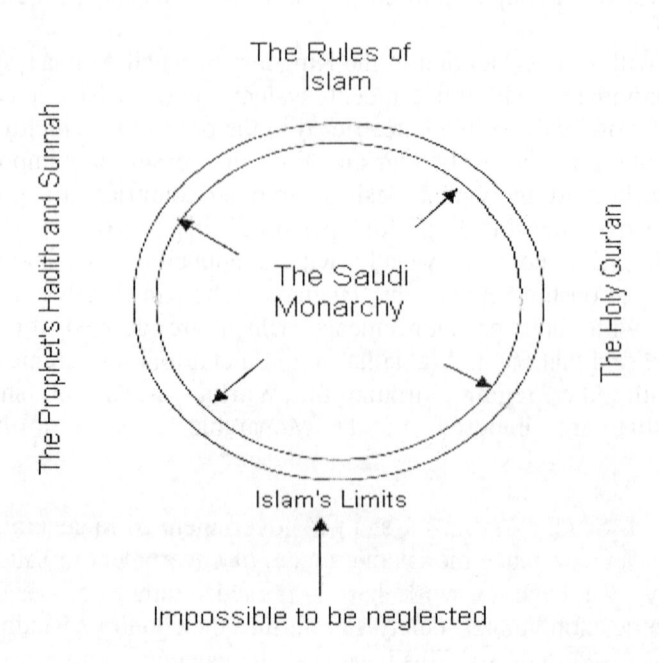

Subjective Law

Other Monarchies

Subjective Law

The Rules of Islam

The Prophet's Hadith and Sunnah

The Saudi Monarchy

The Holy Qur'an

Islam's Limits

Impossible to be neglected

The Open Councils

Justice is the foundation of Governance

5 - 4: Analytical Comparisons

In her Ph.D. Dissertation: "Political Participation in The Arab World: The Mechanism of The Council", Jacqueline Mateka has developed a very good analysis of, and comparison between, the Arab system of government and its Western counterpart[62]:

The emphases of the Arab system:	The emphases of the Western system:
Personalism	Objective Establishments
Non - Separation of the Authorities	Separation of The Authorities
Competition is Unseen	Competition is Seen
Idealism	Realism
Untrustworthiness	Trustworthiness
Unanimous Agreement	Majority Agreement
Religion	Secularisation
Selection is Authenticated	Competitive Elections
Man himself is unable to rule	Rationality of Man
Informal Networks and Networks of Interest	Organisation of Interests
Tribal or Familial Political Social Units	Individualism
The nation is to be united without communities	Multiple and Competitive Communities

Figure (5a) A comparison of Arab and Western government

Although this comparison requires more detailed discussion, it is important to observe from it the point of view of the West, in order to highlight what is interesting for us. These differences are pointed to by means of explaining the four distinctive features of the Kingdom of Saudi Arabia's system of government:

- In Islam, the policies are not formal and fixed. The ruler is an agent of the nation. As a result, he talks on behalf of the ordinary person.
- The sharing is personal. In this system contact is face to face instead of bureaucratic.
- The co-partnership is idealistic: Compromises are reached on material details but the religious rules must be followed.

---

[62] Mateka, Jacquelin "Political Participation in the Arab World: The Majlis Mechanism". Ph.D. thesis presented at University of Texas at Austin 1983.

The Open Councils

- The joint nature of power is achieved by means of "The Open Council" in the process of the policy's decision making, the Saudi citizens prefer Shura over elections.

In addition to the above mentioned, there is another point, regarding the meaning of democracy. It has been changing since its creation. For example, in the book, "Miracle of the Desert"[63], by Ahmad Assah, it has been stated that, in its origin, the term 'democracy' was a Greek word. It meant "government of the people by the people". While, in Grecian society, the word "people" did not mean all the citizens, but one tenth of the Greek population. It consisted of Freemen, while nine tenths of the Greeks were enslaved. For this reason, democracy had not meant Equality for all Greek people. After that, in the European Continent, after the eruption of the French Revolution, "democracy" meant 'Liberty, Brotherhood, and the Equality of all'.

We believe that it is misleading to import foreign expressions concerning democracy to be employed or be compared with the Kingdom of Saudi Arabia's ruling system. For example, if we assume that when Saudi Arabia was established, the ruling system was autocratic - the rule of one person with unlimited power – we would be mistaken, although it might look that way on the surface.

Such a ruling system was unknown in Saudi Arabia. In other words, the late King 'Abdul-'Aziz, during his reign, had taken over the Imamate before he laid claim to royalty. His mission as an Imam was superior to his job as a King. According to Islam, homage resembles Western elections: It includes certain principles and fundamental conditions for whoever is to be recognised as an Imam, or the Head of State. Therefore, the Saudi Kingdom's system of rule as an Islamic regime, does not give the King absolute power, because his duties are specified by Shari'a.

Some people think that the Saudi monarchy resembles other monarchies. In fact, they are mistaken because they believe that the Islamic political system allows the King to dominate his people without actually *governing* them. However, Islam does not accept such a system

---

[63] Assah, Ahmad. *Miracle of the Desert* (Beirut: The Lebanese Domestic Presses, Third Edition, 1971 A.D / 1972 A.D) p. 273.

and recognises the form of government where the King is there to rule as long as his ruling achieves the general welfare of the people.

He remains responsible first of all before Allah, then before his people. The King is responsible for everything in the state, because the ruler in Islam is like the shepherd who is responsible for his flock.

So, is the Kingdom of Saudi Arabia's regime democratic? My opinion consists of the following two points:

1. The concept of the Open Council agrees with the essence of democracy.
2. The ruling system of Saudi Arabia is Islamic rule and therefore contains its own checks and balances for ensuring the welfare of the people.

It seems, in general, that the Western assumption is that Saudi Arabia's regime is undemocratic. But Saudi Arabian writers and other Orientals often say that the Saudi system of rule adheres to the essence of democracy.

5 - 5: Summary

In human society, the form of rule results from numerous factors: geographic, economic, and social, in addition to the beliefs and traditions adopted by the society. As a result, in order to acknowledge the nature of the Kingdom of Saudi Arabia's system of government, you have to realise its background.

Moreover, if we examine Saudi Arabia in this way, we are able to correct misconceptions. Saudi Arabia has a unique history and model of government. We ought to bear this in mind when we compare the Saudi regime with others.

Chapter Six

The Open Councils: Procedures and Functions

6 - 1: Foreword
6 - 2: The Concept of the Council
6 - 3: The History of the Council
6 - 4: The Organisational Structure of the government of the Kingdom of Saudi Arabia
6 - 4 - 1: The King
6 - 4 - 2: The Crown Prince
6 - 4 - 3: The Prime Minister's Second Deputy
6 - 4 - 3: The Council of Ministers
6 - 4 - 4: The Open Councils
6 - 4 - 5 - 1: The types of Open Council
6 - 4 - 5 - 2: Eligibility for membership of the Open Councils
6 - 4 - 5 - 3: Matters discussed in the Council
6 - 4 - 5 - 4: The measures of the Council
6 - 5: The Effectiveness of the Open Councils: An Interview with the Emir of Riyadh
6 - 6: The Results of the Field Study
6 - 7: Summary

6 - 1: Foreword

The relationship between democracy and monarchy is one that is complex and I hope to shed some light on it in this chapter.

6 - 2: The Concept of the Council

In Saudi Arabia the term *Al-Majlis* is used. It refers to the open meeting that is held between government officials and the citizens. The object of this meeting is to give the people an opportunity to air their grievances with officials, so that they might together find solutions, in the manner of members of a family.

In Saudi Arabia, people are proud of their country. It is made very easy for any person to meet the King or any official. This is one of the Open Council's most significant policies, characterised by its simplicity. Everyone attending the Council is equal to each other. From this, some call the Open Council system 'direct democracy' and 'real democracy'. If asked by a foreigner whether they can meet any government official, a Saudi citizen would answer yes.

Before presenting details of the Open Council process, I will present a brief historical background.

6 - 3: The History of the Council

When talking about the Council's history, it is important to know the roots of Islam and its relationship with Arab traditions.

6 - 3 - 1: The Arab background of the Council and its Islamic history.
During his life, Prophet Muhammad (PBUH) used to meet Muslims at the Mosque, as well as in His house, to give teachings about religion, to discuss problems of daily life and ways of overcoming obstacles. The Prophet represented religious and political leadership. After His death Caliphs and other leaders continued this practice. Tribal leaders have their own councils. The strong custom of hospitality dictates that guests are invited to stay in their host's living room.

Another custom is entertaining family and neighbours with generosity. Men and women are entertained separately. The Council system was born out of the tradition of welcome and comfort offered to one's guests.

6 - 4: The Organisational Structure of Saudi Arabia's Government

6 - 4 – 1: The King. The King is Head of State, the Prime Minister and Commander in Chief of all Saudi Arabia's Armed Forces. He is head of the judicial, executive and legislative authorities. He directs internal and foreign policies and is held responsible before Allah and all Muslims.

(The Articles: 5, 44, 50, 52, 55, 56, 58, 60, 64, 64, 68, 69, & 70 of the basic law of government defining his missions as well as duties. (See Appendix No. 5)[64].

6 - 4 - 2: His Royal Highness, The Crown Prince and First Deputy of the Council of Ministers. The Crown Prince is the second most important official in the government. In addition, he is the Viceroy of the King during the King's absence from the country. Sections: C, D, & E of the Fifth Item state the method of choosing the Crown Prince. It also specifies his responsibilities. The King is responsible for selecting him and removing him from his position if necessary. The King directs his work. On the death of the King he takes full responsibility after homage is completed.

6 - 4 - 3: His Royal Highness the Prime Minister's Second Deputy is the third most important man in the government. He takes responsibility if the King and the Crown Prince are absent. (The Fifth Article of the Rule's Basic Legislation.)

6 - 4 - 4: The Cabinet of the Kingdom of Saudi Arabia. Saudi Arabia's Council of Ministers consists of twenty-two ministries: Agriculture; Industry and Electricity; Trade; Communications; Telegraph (Post and Telephone); Defence and Aviation; Education; Finance and National Economy; Foreign Affairs; Health, Higher Education; Public Works and Housing; Interior Affairs; Justice; Labour

---

[64] For more information, see: Al-Baz, Ahmad. *op. cit.* pp. 106 - 108.

The Open Councils

and Social Affairs; Municipal and Rural Affairs; Petroleum and Mineral Resources; Planning; Pilgrimage; Islamic Affairs; Information; Civil Service; as well as seven Ministers of State (i.e. Ministers without Portfolio) (See: Figure No. 6). All the Ministers are Saudis of influence and experience, and include members of the Royal Family.

Because decentralisation is a fundamental characteristic of Saudi Arabian rule, authority is completely divided among the Ministers. Some of them have Deputies, while others have many assistants. In Riyadh, the Council of Ministers holds a meeting once a week, to discuss issues of importance. During Hajj seasons, it holds its regular meetings in Jeddah to serve the Hajjis. Its meetings can be held in any city.

Justice is the foundation of Governance

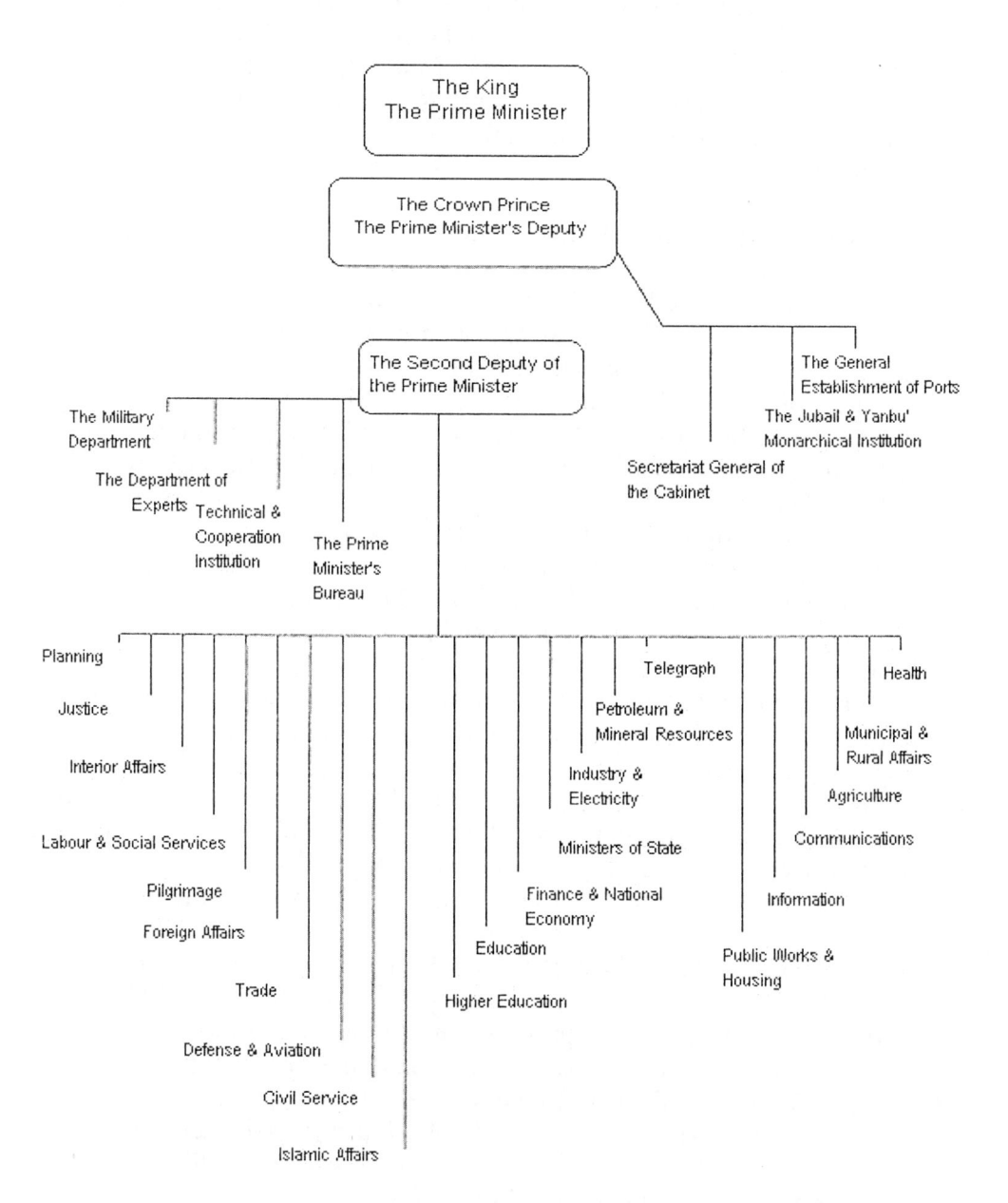

Figure (6): The Council of Ministers of Saudi Arabia.

6 - 4 - 4: Open Councils. The Open Council is the place where officials and citizens can meet. It may be held in the Royal Diwan, The Crown Prince's Bureau, or the offices of the officials. These rooms are suitably large and accommodating. The King and Crown Prince usually meet the people in a large and comfortable hall. Its size is nearly 5000 square feet.

6 - 4 - 5 - 1: The Types of Open Council

1) The Council of the King: In the Royal Diwan, the King meets the people twice a week. He also dines with a group of citizens once a week. He sees the 'Ulama once a week.
2) The Crown Prince's Council: The Crown Prince meets the citizens twice a week. Moreover, he dines with some of them at his home. In addition, he sees the people once a week at the headquarters of the National Guards.
3) The Council of the Second Deputy Prime Minister:
The Second Deputy of the Prime Minister meets the people in the morning and the evening; at his bureau in the Defence and Aviation Ministry, He sees them and in the evening dines with them at his palace.
4) The Council of the Interior Minister or His Deputy is daily, and is often overcrowded because of their close relations with the citizens, especially for local and security issues.
5) The Councils of Ministers and their Deputies (their under-secretaries): The Ministers and their Deputies hold their Councils in their offices, if necessary, for they do not face the same volume of problems faced by the Minister of the Interior or the Administrative Ruler.
6) The Councils of The Province Emirs (i.e. the Administrative Governors): These ministers are attached to the Council: Those governors have had the opportunity of solving the citizens' day-to-day problems, in addition to the issues concerning their bureaux.
7) The Councils of the City Mayors and the Chiefs of the Small Towns and Villages are appointed by the Interior Minister and the Administrative Governor. They have councils similar to the Administrative Governor's (See: Figure No. 7).

Justice is the foundation of Governance

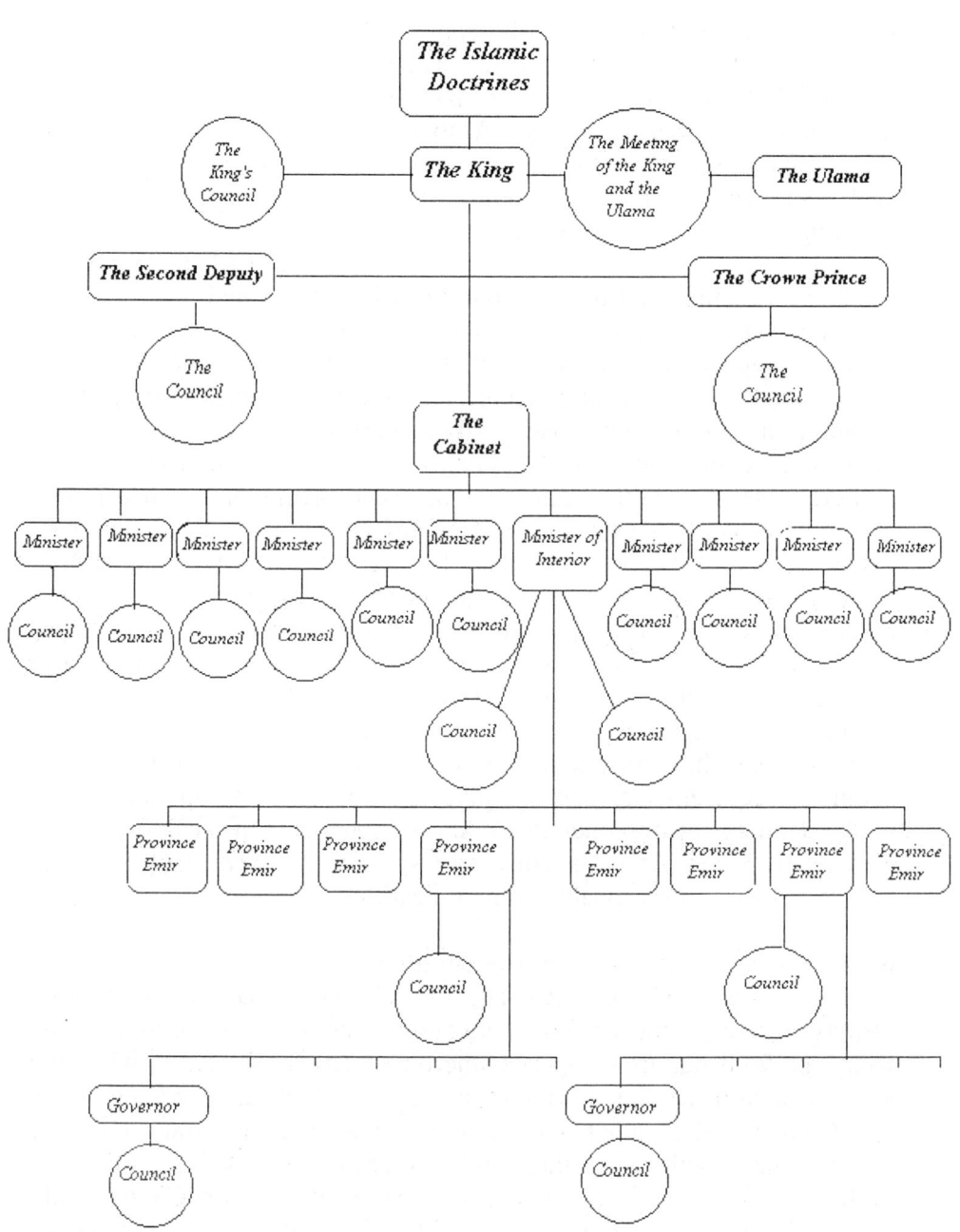

Figure (7): The formation and levels of the Councils

The Open Councils

6 - 4 - 5 - 2: Who goes to the Open Councils and when?

In Saudi Arabia, at any time, all people including foreigners are able to go to the council when they face obstacles. It is not necessary to have a particularly complex problem to have it solved by the governmental institutions. Furthermore, Saudi Arabia's leadership receives telephone calls from any citizen, which is a successful administrative policy. It deals sincerely with these phone calls, day or night, concerning anything related to the citizen or the homeland.

6 - 4 - 5 - 3: The questions discussed inside the Council

In general, all problems can be discussed in the Council, such as: tribal conflicts, security questions (e.g. thefts, robberies, quarrels), as well as social and municipal matters connected to different kinds of properties. In addition, the citizens discuss their personal viewpoints related to politics or confidential needs (such as: asking for monetary aid or seeking help in health matters). The Saudi Kingdom's government officially prohibits criticism of its foreign policies inside the Open Councils, but this does not mean that such criticism is absent, or that external policies are not talked about in the Open Councils. What matters is the way of expression, not it's content. Moreover, the King, his Crown Prince, and all leaders agree about the fundamental truth in the opinions expressed by the citizens. The Kingdom of Saudi Arabia's Government does its best to attract real public points of view, bearing in mind that this information has to be obtained in order to fulfil the people's requirements. The best place of showing those opinions freely is the Council. Consequently, it allows opponents to speak out, while preserving Saudi Arabia's conventions: keeping an organised human society, as well as reasonable communication.

6 - 4 - 5 - 4: The measures of the Council

1. The Council of the Monarch, the Crown Prince, and the Second Deputy Prime Minister: When anybody enters the Council to meet the King, he finds hundreds of seats where he waits for the King, while the King accomplishes his protocol interviews. After that, the King enters the Council's Hall, greets the attendants and sits at the front. Then, he shakes hands with all of them and receives the papers describing their problems. Later on, everyone, especially the Senior Citizens talk personally with him about their troubles. Thereafter, every person sits in the Royal Diwan, in order to have a cup of Arabian coffee, while the

Monarch addresses the people who are present concerning their daily questions. Thereupon, the urgent and significant problems are solved immediately or directed to specialised institutions. The King often asks the person to have a seat in front of him, or beside him, in order to talk about his troubles. If a religious judgement has been issued he is not able to change it. But other simple troubles introduced to the monarch are solved through his Secretary on the same day.

During the absence of the monarch for any reason, the Crown Prince as well as the Second Deputy Prime Minister hold their Councils.

2. The Minister of Interior Affairs or his Deputy: As for the Council, they do the same, but they work hard to overcome all the problems when numerous memorandums from the related ministers are received.

3. The Emirs, the Governors and the Centres' Chiefs hold councils with differences in position and protocol procedures. The measures are simpler than higher level Councils.

There is another difference between the Minister's Council and the Administrative Ruler's: There are assistants who make sure they have the correct details of a problem. For example, if there is an issue, which needs more inspection, one of the assistants is sent by the minister or the Administrative Governor, to gather more information and return quickly with the findings. Then, the solution to the problem is implemented.

6 - 5: The Open Council's Effectiveness: An Interview with the Emir of Riyadh

In order to have an official's point of view concerning the Council I interviewed His Royal Highness Prince Salman bin 'Abdul 'Aziz, who has been the Emir of the Riyadh District since 1373 AH/1954 AD. Everyday, he meets approximately one thousand people from all levels in one of the most important regions of the Kingdom of Saudi Arabia. Below is His Royal Highness' replies to my questions.

Q: When did the Council commence in Saudi Arabia?
A: As a matter of fact it is Islamic heritage: The Prophet Muhammad (PBUH) used to meet the people at the Nabawi Mosque. Because our

homeland is Islamic, it has adhered to this tradition since the epoch of THE First Saudi Kingdom. Consequently, we thank Allah the Almighty for this tradition.

Q: What is the Council's intention within Saudi Arabia?
A: As I have already mentioned, the Saudi people as well as those is positions of responsibility in the Kingdom have been accustomed to the Council. It aims at making the citizens and the ministers close to each other. For this reason, according to my personal experience, it is an essential social mechanism.

Q: Is the Open Council a Law or a System?
A: It is neither. But, there are directions issued by the Custodian of the Two Holy Mosques King Fahd in his speech to the citizens.

Q: What do you think about your meetings with the people? What is going on inside the Council?
A: Lots of discussions and arguments take place among its attendees. These things are necessary for the officials, because they become capable of knowing what is occurring within their human society. In addition, everything has advantages as well as disadvantages. Nevertheless, I do think that its positive aspects are more than its negative ones. Furthermore, the governmental institutions spend a lot of time and effort on it; the citizens want that.

Q: What do you call it? Do you look at it as a form of direct democracy?
A: Surely, yes: When comparing it with the West's ideas, I can say that it is a kind of direct democracy, for you are able to see the people discussing directly with leaders in order to solve their problems.

Q: Do you suppose that the citizens of the Kingdom of Saudi Arabia are satisfied when they meet the leaders?
A: The majority of them accept the decisions made in the Council. But like all countries there are people who are dissatisfied with the outcome of the meeting.

Q: Do you assume that it is a fundamental organisation of Saudi Arabia as a modern state, when it is viewed as a way of listening to the citizens?

A: I think that it is important for it to continue forever. Although I come across a lot of difficulties as a leader, but I believe that it is extremely good for me as a means to accomplish all my missions; it is much better than bureaucracy.

Q: Will Saudi Arabia's government develop it in order to fit with modern requirements?
A: In fact we are developing through the course of time. Moreover, the problems we are presented with are becoming ever more diverse and complicated. Further, there is greater awareness of how to use governmental institutions to overcome problems. The Bedouins and villagers still come to the Council to solve simple problems. So, as the level of the citizens' awareness and education increases, their utilisation of the Council decreases.

Q: What are the types of problems presented to the Council?
A: The main varieties of problems presented are confidential problems and ones related to property and the tribes. We often discuss matters of policy as a way of gauging public opinion.

Q: If a person were to take his problem to the governor but the governor fails to solve it, is the person able to meet higher officials or the King?
A: Yes, of course. King Fahd said that if anyone does not accept the solution, then he is able to meet the Interior Minister, the Crown Prince or the Monarch himself. Also, the people can go to the Chief of Justice's Diwan or the Investigation Administration where they can complain or take legal actions against the responsible persons. They always meet the representatives of these institutes in order to ask about specified points.

Q: Do you consider it as one of the success factors of Saudi Arabia's government?
A: Yes. It is a foundation of Saudi Arabia's ruling system. It continually works hard to close the gap between officials and the citizens. People and officials meet face to face to solve problems and can consult any other responsible persons. The administrative rulers of any area within the Saudi Kingdom are all happy to help any needy person. We praise Allah for the strong co-operation that exists between the Saudi people and the government.

Q: Is its system confined to a certain social class of people?
A: It is for all of the citizens, whether they are Saudi or foreign residents. In addition, officials are dealt with as ordinary employees. Anyone in the Kingdom of Saudi Arabia knows well that he can get justice from the Council.

6 - 6: The Results of the Field Study

In order to discover the Saudi People's points of view concerning the Council, the writer carried out some field research. Three hundred adults at the Council were questioned (see Appendix 3). This survey was carried out in the Emirate of Riyadh.
The results are as follows:

Question One: The problems presented:
50 % Confidential
10 % Municipal
10 % Formal (i.e. Governmental)
20 % Financial
5 % Tribal
5 % Hygienic

Question Two: The reasons for attending the Council:
50 % to make problems known to the leaders
30 % to obtain a settlement in a faster fashion than the Government's routine measures offer
20 % to gain the justice of the King or Prince, which is assumed to be sound and trustworthy

Question Three: The difficulty of attendance:
100% state that they have not come across any obstacles in presenting their problems

Question Four: The number of visits to the Council
65 % have attended more than once (Naturally, the percentage of attendants at Prince Salman's Council is high because it has existed for 40 years and has received, every day, hundreds of visitors.)
10 % have attended once before
25 % have visited for the first time in their lives

Question Five: The kind of solution:
50 % reported that it is just
45 % said that it is satisfactory
5 % did not respond

Question Six: Opinions concerning the Council:
90 % stated that it is very good
10 % reported that it is acceptable

Question Seven: The alternative:
30 % have chosen Shari'a
50 % have chosen to renew the complaint
20 % said that they would resort to a higher council

Question Eight: The easiness of meeting the officials:
100 % reported that they found it easy to meet with officials

Question Nine: The necessity of making an appointment:
92 % did not require an appointment
3 % made an appointment
5 % did not go to the Monarch's Council

Question Ten: The speed of response:
67 % were satisfied
28 % found that it varied from time to time
5 % were not satisfied

Question Eleven: Do people go themselves or entrust the duty to others?
100 % stated that they prefer to go themselves to the Council in order to overcome their difficulties.

Question Twelve: The extent of satisfaction:
93 % said excellent
5 % said good
2 % said satisfactory

Most of the suggestions of those sampled emphasise the importance of creating a special department in the Council to make sure official decisions are implemented by the administration.

6 - 7: Summary

As Western societies are proud of their Parliaments and democratic systems, so Saudi Arabia's people and government feel proud of the Open Council system. It is regarded as a very efficient channel between the rulers and the ruled, and comes out of age-old Saudi tradition. People are accustomed to allowing officials to guide them in the solution of their personal affairs because they share these traditions. The Council enforces the guidance of Islam, the laws and customs of the society. Within this it encourages the personal aspirations of the people.

Those fulfilling the many and various functions of government are on the same level of the social hierarchy and share the common task of serving the needs of citizens to the best of their ability. There is no rigid class structure in Saudi Arabia.

The Council system, therefore, perfectly meets the expectations and needs of the society of Saudi Arabia and has done so for a century.

Chapter Seven

Results and Expectations

7 - 1: Results
7 - 2: Expectations

7 - 1: Results

This book has concentrated on describing and analysing the Council system in the government of Saudi Arabia. In spite of the extensive previous discussion there remains the interesting question of whether Saudi Arabia is a democratic system.

If the main stipulation of democracy is that government must be determined by direct public election then it is clear that Saudi Arabia is not a democracy.

There are many reasons why there are no public elections in Saudi Arabia:

> 1 - Education is an important factor in determining a country's type of government. In Saudi Arabia it would seem that public elections are not practical. The tribal nature of Saudi society means that Western democratic systems would be manipulated by different tribal factions. This manipulation would affect public elections. Democracy is not the only means to safeguard the interests of the citizens.
>
> Saudi Arabia's monarchy acts as a practical substitute for public elections. There are many positive advantages to monarchy, given the history and society of Saudi Arabia, that are not available in Western systems. For this reason I argue that public elections are not a useful system for Saudi Arabia. Every society evolves its own system of government that suits its circumstances and demographic characteristics. Democracy in the 'developed' nations has also evolved through political and social processes. Saudi Arabia's system is in a state of evolution too.
>
> An example of this is the Shura system that was only approved after a long period of research. Another is the new form of the Ministers' Council system. This

system is not found anywhere else in the world. This system defines the length of time that an official can remain in the Cabinet. This period is 4 years, after which a new appointment is made. (See Appendix 6) This is different in democracies in the West where a Minister can remain in office as long as the ruling party remains in government.

2 - The character of Arab culture is different from Western culture. Saudi people are difficult to target with mass media in the way people in the West are. Hence Western ideas have not spread widely in the Kingdom.

3 - It is frequently supposed that there is no freedom in Saudi Arabia. This is an example of the false accusations, highlighted by Edward Said in his book "Orientalism". In response to this, I argue that in Saudi Arabia there is personal, economic, and social freedom resulting from Islam. The Saudis and their leaders are proud of Saudi Arabia's security and peace and the implementation of Shari'a.

4 - The Saudi Kingdom has observed the results of attempting to adopt Western-style democracy in neighbouring countries. In many of these cases, this form of democracy did not suit the native population. Saudi Arabia was able to come up with a system which preserved the liberties of the people whilst acknowledging traditions of rule. Consequently, a literal adoption of the system of public elections would threaten the achievements of the Saudis.

5 - The writer has made his hypothesis clear in relation to historico-cultural comparisons. He assumes that the public is the best judge of the ruling system most suitable for them. Saudi people are satisfied with their government.

6 - The Saudi system of rule is not static as some have supposed, but has developed and will continue developing step by step through accurate review of the basic ruling system, issued in the form of the Royal Decree No. (A /90), Dt. 27/8/1412 AH / 2/3/1992 AD, we can see modernisation in the ruling system.

7 - The systems of rule were modernised in Royal Decree (A/90), Dt. 2 /8 /1412 AH / 6/2/1992 AD. Furthermore, the system of the Ministers' Council, issued on 3/3/1414 AH / 21/8/1993, is living proof of good administration, especially in providing opportunities for citizens to serve the country, as the period of the council's membership is only four years, when a decree from the ruler establishes a new council.

7 - 2: Expectations

This book shows us the Open Councils' significance. I would argue that the system is in need of enlargement to accommodate changing demographic conditions and to continue this unique aspect as an Arabic and Islamic tradition. This institution, if it is persevered with, will maintain the balance between modern governmental needs and Arab Islamic traditions. I also argue that the government should establish a special department to observe the Council's function and record the issues and resolutions for it and take a census of its users and their demographics. In addition, an Office of the Open Councils for in-depth research should be formed.

Moreover, Saudi Arabia's government should make the Council and its work more widely known to the Saudi population through the mass media in order that it might be of benefit to them.

I am looking forward to seeing the Saudi government sharing with the world her success and stability, especially the capacity for direct communication with senior officials, namely, the system of the Open Councils. Then perhaps some Third World countries can apply a few aspects of this system in their own governmental institutions.

Further, I hope that in the near future the Saudi Kingdom will enter more fully into the international arena, in order to be able to encourage the global community to perceive that:

1. Religion and politics need not be antagonistic and that religion can be an effective base for a system of rule. Saudi Arabia's security and justice are a shining example of this happy marriage.

2. Internal peace has been achieved in Saudi Arabia due to its adherence to Islamic doctrines, which confer honour upon men. Saudi Arabia is eager to see peace throughout the world.

3. Technology and Islam do not contradict one another. As a result, society is able to employ technology whilst maintaining its cultural background.

4. Direct contact with the responsible persons, as well as reaching a great deal of stability is in the people's will. The Council itself is an effective means of achieving this.

5. Like the United States of America, the Kingdom of Saudi Arabia represents a model of governance, to be followed by other, similar countries.

Saudi Arabia has achieved development and prosperity only by remaining faithful to Islam. Moreover, the monarchy does its best to open itself to a world that is short of solutions, in order to offer both practical help, and to stay in touch with the needs of its people.

Bibliography

Arabic References

Al-Baz, Ahmad: *Development Of The Political And Administrative System Inside The Saudi Arabia* (Riyadh: Al-Shibl Publishing House, 1417 AH/1993 AD).

Al-Faisal, Khalid: *The Development And An Eyewitness* (Abha, Mazen Presses, 1419 AH/1998 AD).

Al-Jahni, Eid: *The Kingdom Of Saudi Arabia's Cabinet* (Riyadh: Al-Majed Press, 1984 AD)

Al-Mudawi. Abu Al-'Ala. *The Way Of The Islamic Life* (Riyadh: The Press Of The Administration's Presidency For: The Islamic Studies, Giving The Formal Legal Advisory Opinions, The Mission, As Well As The Guidance, 1984 AD).

Al-Oheideb, 'Abdul-'Aziz. *The Phenomenon Of Security During King Abdul 'Aziz's Reign.* (Riyadh: Al-Isha'a Printing Shop, 1977 AD).

Al-Qabba, Abdullah. *The Foreign Policy Of The Kingdom Of Saudi Arbia* (Riyadh: Al Farazdaq Press, 1986 AD).

Al-Sa'ud, 'Abdullah. *State and Economy Inside The Kingdom Of Saudi Arabia, The Introductory Remarks to The Forum Of Saudi Arabia's Economy & Rule* (The Arabian Gulf Studies Centre, July / 1980 AD).

Al-Sa'ud, Talal bin 'Abdul-'Aziz. *Images Of King 'Abdul-'Aziz's Life.* (Riyadh: Al-Fakhiria Publications and Al-Kitab Al-Arabi Publication House, Beirut: 1405 AH / 1985 AD, Second Edition).

Al-Zarkali, Khair Al Din. *The Manual Of Monarch 'Abdul-'Aziz's Biography*, (Beirut: Dar El-Ilm Lilmalayin, Beirut 1991 A.D, The Seventh Edition).

Assah, Ahmed. *Miracle of the Dessert* (Beirut: Lebanon's Domestic Presses, The Third Edition, 1971 / 1972 AD).

Dahlan, Ahmed. *A Research into Saudi Arabia's Internal Policy* (Jeddah, Al Shurouk Publication House, 1984 AD).

King Fahd: *My Door Is Open For Everybody* (Arab News Newspaper, Issue No. 20, January 1988 AD).

Ibn Taymiyyah, Taqi Al-Din Ahmad bin Abdul-Halim. *Legal Policy* (Riyadh: The General Presidency Of Ordering With Kindness And The Forbidding Of Wrong 1412 AH/1992 AD).

Zeidan, 'Abdul-Karim. *The Fundamentals Of The Mission* (Beirut, Baghdad, Al-Rissala Establishment, Al-Quds Bookshop, The Second Edition, 1407 AH/1987 AD).

Encyclopaedias
The Encyclopaedia Of King 'Abdul-'Aziz: Saudi Arabia In A Hundred Years (Riyadh: Al 'Obaikan Bookshop 1419 AH / 1999 AD).

The World Arab Encyclopaedia (Riyadh: The Establishment Of Encyclopaedia Works For Publishing & Distribution, 1417 AH/1993 AD).

Official documents
Kingdom of Saudi Arabia, The Ministers' Council, The Circular Note No. 22301, (Riyadh: The Cabinet Press 1981 AD).

The Monarchical Decree Law No. 2716 Dt. 17 Jumada Al-Ula 1351 AH / 1932 AD

Umm Al-Qura (1508) On 21/7/1373AH / 26/3/1954 AD, and Umm Al-Qura (1717) On 27/10/1377 AH / 16/5/1958 AD.

Umm Al-Qura, Issue No. 406 Dt. 22 Jumada Al-Ula 1351 AH.

The Royal Act No. (A / 13), On 3/3/1414 AH / 21/8/1993 AD.

Foreign References

Al-Hamad, Hamad Sadun, *"The Legislative Process and the Development of Saudi Arabia"* (Ph.D. diss., University of South California, 1973).

Al-Saud, Mashaal, *"Permanence and Change: An Analysis of the Islamic Political Culture of Saudi Arabia with Special Reference to the Royal Family"* (Ph.D. diss, Claremont Graduate School, 1982).

Al-Seflan, Ali M. *"The Essence of Tribal Leaders Participation, Responsibilities, and Decisions in Some Local Government Activities in Saudi Arabia"* (Ph.D. diss, Claremont Graduate School, 1981).

Area Handbook, Saudi Arabia: A Country Study (Washington D.C.: Headquarters, Department of the Army, 1984).

Assah, Ahmed. *Miracle of the Desert Kingdom*. (London: Johnson Publications, 1969).

Hobday, Peter. *Saudi Arabia Today* (London: Macmillan Press, 1986).

Huyette, Summer Scott. *Political Adaptation in Saudi Arabia* (Boulder, Colo., Westview press, 1985).

Iqbal, Muhammad. *Saudi Arabia: Its Founding and Development* (Kashmir: Jagowal Printing Press, 1986).

Khadduri, Majid. *Arab Contemporaries, the Roles of Personalities in Politics* (Baltimore: John Hopkins University Press, 1973).

Lipsky, George A, *Saudi Arabia: Its People, Its Society, Its Culture* (New Heban: HRAF Press, 1959).

Mateka, Jacquelin *"Political Participation in the Arab World: The Majlis Mechanism"* (Ph.D. thesis presented at University of Texas at Austin 1983).

Nader, Laura. *"Orientalism, Occidentalism and the Control of Women"* (Ph.D. thesis presented at Harvard University, March 1988).

Niblock, Tim. State, *Society and Economy in Saudi Arabia* (New York: St. Martin's Press, 1981).

Rashid, Naser and Esber, Shaheen. *King Fahd and Saudi Arabia's Great Evolution* (Joplin, Mo.: International Institute of Technology, 1987).

Said, Edward. *Orientalism* (New York: Random House, 1979).

Appendices

Appendix 1: A note circulated by the Custodian of the two Holy Mosques when he was a deputy of the Prime Minister, concerning the importance of the 'open door' policy.

Appendix 2: The System of the Shura Council

Appendix 3: The Questionnaire

Appendix 4: The Law of the Provinces

Appendix 5: The Basic Law of Government

Appendix 6: The Cabinet System

Appendix 1:

A note circulated by King Fahd, the Custodian of the two Holy Mosques, when he was Deputy Prime Minister, concerning the importance of the 'open door' policy

Kingdom of Saudi Arabia   No. 217 42301
The Cabinet Diwan   Dt. 2/10/1401 A.H (3/8/1981 AD)
The Administration of Employees and Activities

A Circulated Note

His Royal Highness, the Second Deputy of the Prime Minister and Commander of the National Guard
After regards

We saw His Royal Highness' letter, the Minister of Defence and Aeronautics, the Ministerial Committee's Head of studying some Functional Phenomena, No. 3/41/6 Dt. 10/9/1401 A.H / 12/7/1981 AD. According to this committee's discussions during two sessions held on: 7/7/1401 AH / 12/5/1981 AD & 13/7/1401 AH / 18/5/1981 AD, the members have decided it is vital to reinforce the concept of self-evaluation in governmental institutions. In addition to its positive effects in enhancing responsibility, it is a protective procedure, which prevents administrative and financial contravention. It has to be considered that:
1 - The Minister and the high ranking officials ought to visit unannounced all of the governmental administrations from time to time to observe the processes of work and solve any problem these administrations might face.
2 - The Minister and high-ranking officials have to dedicate no less than sixty minutes every day to receiving people, in order to listen to their complaints and solve their problems. Through these complaints the administration involved can be recognised and the problems can be investigated in order to solve the difficulties faced.
3 - The Minister and the high-ranking officials and the state ministers are to have timetables for accomplishing each service presented by the ministry or the Governmental Administration.
4 - The Minister and the high ranking officials must send reports to the Prime Minister from time to time, outlining their achievements during a particular period. The report should explain the percentage of

achievement according to the plan of the ministry or the Governmental Administration.
We ask that you implement these decisions.
The Prime Minister's Deputy

Appendix 2

The Law of the Shura Council

No. A / 91 Dt. 27 / 8/ 1412 A.H.

By Almighty Allah's will, We, Fahd bin 'Abdul-'Aziz Al Sa'ud, the Monarch of Saudi Arabia, according to Allah's words: {**And consult with them upon the conduct of affairs**}, and His words: {**and whose affairs are a matter of counsel**}, and following Allah's Messenger (PBUH) in consulting his companions, and depending on the public benefit.

And after looking into the Shura Council's system, issued by Monarchical Ordinance in 1347 AH,
Have decided upon the following:
A.   The issuing of a new system for the Shura Council.
B.   The new system will replace the one issued in 1347 AH.
C.   All legislation and decisions, declared in the past, continue to be in effect until notice of further revision or amendment according to the new system.
D.   It will be in effect within six months of its publication.
E.   It is to be published in the Official Gazette (Umm Al-Qura).

The Law of the Shura Council

Article 1
In compliance with the words of Almighty Allah: {**It was by the mercy of Allah that thou wast lenient with them (O Muhammad), for if thou hadst been stern and fierce of heart they would have dispersed from round about thee. So pardon them and ask forgiveness for them and consult with them upon the conduct of affairs. And when thou art resolved, then put thy trust in Allah. Lo! Allah loveth those who put their trust (in Him)**} And his other word: {**And those who answer the call of their Lord and establish worship, and whose affairs are a matter of counsel, and who spend of what We have**

bestowed on them} And following the Sunnah of his Messenger who consulted his companions and urged the nation to engage in consultation, the Shura Council shall be established to exercise all tasks entrusted to it according to this law and the basic law of government while adhering to the Book of Allah and the Sunnah of the Messenger maintaining brotherly ties and co-operating in kindness and piety.

Article 2
The Shura Council shall hold fast to the rope of Allah and pledge itself to the sources of Islamic legislation. All members of the Shura Council shall ever serve in the public interest and shall preserve the unity of the community, the entity of the state and the interest of the nation.

Article 3
The Shura Council shall consist of a chairman and ninety members chosen by the King from among the scholars and men of knowledge, expertise and specialisation. Their duties and all other affairs shall be defined by royal order.

Article 4
It is stipulated that every member of Shura Council shall be:
- A Saudi national by birth and descent,
- A competent person of recognised good character
- Not younger than 30 years of age.

Article 5
Any member may submit a request to resign his membership to the Chairman of the Shura Council, who in turn shall refer it to the King.

Article 6
If a member of the Shura Council neglects the duties of his work he shall be investigated and tried according to rules and measures to be issued by royal order.

Article 7
If a member's place in the Shura Council becomes vacant for any reason, the King shall choose a replacement and issue a royal order to this effect.

Article 8
No member of the Shura Council shall exploit his membership for his own interest.

Article 9
Membership of the Shura Council shall not be combined with any governmental post, or with the management of any company, unless the King deems it necessary.

Article 10
The Chairman, his Deputy and the Secretary General of the Shura Council shall be appointed and relieved by royal orders. Their salaries, duties and all their other affairs shall be defined by a royal order.

Article 11
Prior to assumption of their duties, the Chairman, the Members and the Secretary General of the Shura Council shall take the following oath before the King:
"I swear by Almighty Allah to be loyal to my religion, then to my King and country I swear not to reveal any of the secrets of state, to protect its interests and laws and to perform my duties with sincerity, integrity, loyalty and fairness.

Article 12
The city of Riyadh is the seat of the Shura Council. The Shura Council may convene in another area within the Kingdom if the King deems it necessary.

Article 13
The fixed term of the Shura Council shall be four years, effective from the date of the royal order issued for the formation of the Council. A new Council shall be formed at least two months before the end of the current Council's term. If the term expires before the formation of the new Council, the previous one shall remain active until a new Council is formed. When a new Council is formed, the number of the newly selected members shall not be less than 50% of the entire Council's members.

Article 14
The King, or whomever he appoints as deputy, shall deliver an annual royal speech to the Shura Council on the domestic and foreign policy of the State.

Article 15
The Shura Council shall express its opinion on the general policies of the state referred to it by the Prime Minister, specifically, the Council shall have the right to do the following:
Discuss the general plan for economic and social development.
Study laws and bylaws, international treaties and agreements, and concessions, and make whatever suggestions it deems appropriate.
Interpret laws.
Discuss annual reports forwarded by ministries and other governmental institutions, and make whatever suggestions it deems appropriate.

Article 16
No meeting held by the Shura Council shall be considered official without a quorum of at least two thirds of its members, including the Chairman or his Deputy. Resolutions shall not be considered official without majority approval.

Article 17
The resolutions of the Shura Council shall be forwarded to the Prime Minister. If the views of both councils are in agreement, the resolutions shall come into force following the King's approval. If the views are in disagreement, the King may decide what he deems appropriate.

Article 18
Laws, international treaties and agreements, and concessions shall be issued and amended by royal decrees after being studied by the Shura Council.

Article 19
The Shura Council shall form specialised committees from amongst its members to exercise the powers within its jurisdiction. The Council may also form other specialised committees to discuss any items on the agenda.

Article 20
The Shura Council's committees may seek the help of others who are not members of the Council, with the Chairman's approval.

Article 21
The Shura Council shall have a general commission composed of the Chairman, his Deputy and the heads of the specialised committees.

Article 22
The Chairman of Shura Council shall submit requests to the Chairman of the Council of Ministers to summon any government official to the meeting of Shura Council when matters relating to his jurisdiction are discussed. The official shall have the right to debate but not the right to vote.

Article 23
Any group of ten members of the Shura Council have the right to propose a new draft law or an amendment to a law already in force and submit it to the chairman of the Council. The Chairman shall submit the proposal to the King.

Article 24
The chairman of the Shura Council shall submit a request to the Prime Minister to provide the Council with information and documents in the

processions of government institutions, which the Council believes, are necessary to facilitate its work.

Article 25

The Chairman of the Shura Council shall submit an annual report to the King on its work in accordance with the Council by-law.

Article 26

Civil service laws shall apply to employees of the secretariat of the Council unless its bylaws stipulate to the contrary.

Article 27

The Shura Council shall be allocated a special budget to be approved by the King. It shall be spent in accordance with rules to be issued by royal order.

Article 28

The Shura Council's financial matters and the auditing and closing of accounts shall be carried out in accordance with special rules to be issued by royal order.

Article 29

The bylaws of the Shura Council shall define the functions of the Chairman of the Shura Council, his Deputy, the Secretary General of the Council, the Secretariat, the methods of conducting its sessions, the management of its work and its committees' work and the voting procedure. The regulations shall also specify rules of debate, the forms of response and other procedures conducive to restraint and discipline within the Council. It shall exercise its powers for the good of the Kingdom and the prosperity of its people. These regulations shall be issued by royal order.

Article 30

This law can be amended only in the same manner in which it was promulgated.

THE BY-LAWS OF THE SHURA COUNCIL

No. A / 15 Dt. 03 / 03/ 1412 A.H.

With the help of Allah, We, Fahd bin 'Abdul-'Aziz Al-Sa'ud, Monarch of the Kingdom of Saudi Arabia, having reviewed THE LAW OF SHURA COUNCIL issued by Royal Order No. A/91 and dated 27/8/1412H,
Order the following:
A.   Issuing of:

1. THE BY-LAWS OF THE SHURA COUNCIL as included.
2. BY-LAWS ON THE RIGHTS AND DUTIES of Members of the Shura Council as included.
3. Rules of Financial and Personnel Affairs
4. Rules and Procedures for Investigation and Trial of Shura Council Members
B. Those two rules and two bylaws are to be published in the gazette and to be in effect from the date of this order

THE BY-LAWS OF THE SHURA COUNCIL

Chapter One
Jurisdiction of the Chairman of the Council, His Deputy and the Secretary General

Article 1
The chairman of the Council shall supervise all functions of the Council, shall represent it at other agencies and organisations and shall be its spokesman.

Article 2
The Chairman of the Council shall head all sessions of the Council and the steering committee as well as any committee meetings he attends.

Article 3
The Chairman of the Shura Council shall open and close Council sessions, chair meetings, moderate and participate in deliberations, give the floor to speakers, specify the topic for discussion, draw the attention of speakers to the time limit and the subject matter of discussion, end discussions and move motions. He may do whatever he deems necessary to maintain order during sessions.

Article 4
The chairman of the Shura Council may call the Council, the Steering Committee or any other committee for an emergency meeting to discuss a specific topic.

Article 5
The Deputy Chairman of the Shura Council shall assist the Chairman in his presence and assume his duties in his absence.

Article 6
The Deputy Chairman shall preside over Council and Steering Committee sessions when the chairman is absent, and in case both are absent whosoever is designated by the King shall preside over the

Council. The Deputy Chairman and the King's designee shall have the same jurisdiction as those specified for the Chairman.
Article 7
The Secretary General or whosoever represents him shall attend the Council and Steering Committee sessions. He shall supervise the taking of the minutes and announce the schedule and the agenda of the sessions. In addition he shall attend to all duties assigned by the Council, by the Steering Committee or by the Chairman of the Council. He shall answer to the Chairman of the Council for all the financial and administrative affairs to the Council.

Chapter Two
The Steering Committee of the Council

Article 8
The Steering Committee shall consist of the Chairman of the Council, his Deputy and heads of specialised committees.
Article 9
A Steering Committee meeting shall not be official unless attended by at least two-thirds of the members. It shall pass resolutions by majority vote. In case of a tie, the Chairman shall cast the deciding vote.
Article 10
The minutes of every meeting of the Steering Committee shall indicate the time and place of the meeting, the names of those present, the names of those absent, a synopsis of the deliberations and the full text of the recommendations. The minutes shall be signed by the Chairman of the Council and attending members.
Article 11
The Steering Committee shall have authority over the following:
The preparation of a general plan for the Council and its committees to enable it to realise its objectives.
The preparation of an agenda for the Council meetings.
The reaching of final decisions regarding objections to the minutes of a session, the result of pooling, the counting of votes or any other objections raised during sessions and its decision in this regard shall be final.
The making of rules of procedure for the Council and its committees in accordance with the rules and regulations of the Council.

Chapter Three
Session

Article 12
The Shura Council shall hold one ordinary session at least once a fortnight. The Chairman shall decide the date and time of the sessions. The Chairman may advance or postpone sessions when necessary.

Article 13
The agenda of a session shall be distributed to all members ahead of time along with reports pertaining to agenda items and whatever else the Steering Committee of the Council deems necessary.

Article 14
Members of the Shura Council must study the items on the agenda on the premises of the Council, and he shall never, under any circumstances, take any papers, draft laws or documents related to his work outside the premises of the Council.

Article 15
A member shall submit in writing a request to address the Council during sessions, and requests shall be honoured in order of receipt.

Article 16
The Chairman shall allow a member to speak, taking into consideration the order of receipt of his request and the public interest.

Article 17
A member shall not speak on a single topic for more than ten minutes, unless allowed otherwise by the Chairman. A member shall only address the Chairman of the Council, and none but the Chairman shall be allowed to interrupt the member.

Article 18
The Council may postpone or restudy a certain topic, and the Chairman may temporarily adjourn for no more than one hour.

Article 19
Each session shall be recorded in minutes which state the venue and date of the session, the time it started, the name of the chairman, the number of members present, the names of those absent, and the reasons for their absences, if any, a summary of discussions, the numbers of those voting in favour and those voting against, the result of the voting, the texts of resolutions, all that is related to the postponement or suspension of the session and the time of its adjournment, as well as any other matters the Chairman deems necessary.

Article 20
The Chairman of the Council as well as the Secretary General or his Deputy shall sign the minutes after they are read to the members, and any member has the right to study them if he wishes.

Chapter Four
Committees

Article 21
The Shura Council shall, at the outset of each term, form the necessary specialised committees from among the Council members to exercise its jurisdiction.

Article 22
Each specialised committee shall be formed of a number of members to be determined by the Council, provided the number is not less than five. The Council shall also name these members, the Committee Chairman and his Deputy, taking into consideration members' qualifications and committee needs. The Council shall also form ad hoc committees to study certain issues, and each of the specialised committees can form sub-committees from among its members to study specific issues.

Article 23
The Council may reconstitute its specialised committees and form new ones.

Article 24
A committee chairman shall manage the work of the committee and speak on its behalf before the Council. When the Chairman is absent, his Deputy shall take over. The most senior committee member chairs the committee when the Chairman and his Deputy are absent.

Article 25
A committee meets upon the call of the committee Chairman, the Council or the Chairman of the Council.

Article 26
Committee meetings shall be held in camera, and they shall not be considered legal unless a minimum of two thirds of the committee members is present. Each committee shall write down its agenda upon its Chairman's request, and shall issue its recommendation by the majority of the members present. The Chairman's vote shall cast the deciding vote when votes are equal.

Article 27
A committee shall study whatever issues are referred to it by the Council or the Chairman of the Council, and if the issue concerns more than one committee, the Chairman shall decide which committee studies the issue first or may refer it to a joint committee of all the members of the committee concerned under the chairmanship of the Chairman of the Council or his Deputy.

Article 28
Any Council member may express his opinion on any issue that has been referred to one of the specialised committees, even if he is not a member of that committee, provided that he presents his opinion in writing to the chairman of the Council.

Article 29
Minutes shall be taken of each committee meeting, stating the date and venue of the meeting, the names of members present and absent, a summary of the discussions and the text of its recommendations. The Chairman and the members present shall sign the minutes.

Article 30
When study of a certain issue is complete, a committee shall write a report that explains the issue, the committee's point of view, its recommendations and their bases. If there is a minority point of view it shall also be included.

Chapter Five
Voting and Adoption of Resolutions

Article 31
Council resolutions shall be adopted by majority as provided by article 16 of the Law of the Shura Council. In case a majority is not achieved, the issue shall be scheduled for voting in the next session. In the event of the issue not winning a majority in the second session, the issue shall be referred to the King along with whatever studies have been completed concerning it, as well as the results of voting in both sessions.

Article 32
No deliberations or presentations of new opinions shall be allowed during the voting process. In all cases, the Chairman should cast his vote after all the members have voted.

Chapter Six
General Provisions

Article 33
The Chairman of the Shura Council shall submit his annual report as provided in Article 25 of the Law of the Council within the first three months of the New Year. This report shall include all the studies and projects carried out in the previous year in addition to all resolutions passed and the current status of all pending issues.

Article 34
The financial and personnel affairs of the Council shall be managed in accordance with the bylaws regulating the Council's financial and personnel affairs.
The Chairman of the Council shall issue the rules necessary for regulating the financial and administrative functions of the Council, including the organisational hierarchy, and the tasks of the various officers of the Council, in accordance with the law of the Council and its by-laws.

By-laws on the rights and duties of Members of the Shura Council

Article 1
Membership of the Shura Council shall take effect from the beginning of the Council's term as specified in the order for its formation according to Article 13 of the Law of the Council. A substitute member's term of office shall commence on the date specified in the royal order nominating him and shall expire at the end of the Council's term. In case the term of the Council should end before the new Council is formed, his membership shall remain valid until the new Council is formed, unless his membership is terminated.

Article 2
The member of the Shura Council shall receive a monthly remuneration of SR 20.000 during his term of office and shall be treated like a 15th grade employee as far as allowances, compensations, privileges and increments are concerned. All this shall not affect the pension that a member may deserve.

Article 3
A full time Council member shall retain the position and grade he held before joining the Council. His term of office in the Council shall be taken into consideration with respect to merit increases, promotions and

retirement. A member shall pay, during membership, his pension premiums according to his basic salary.

A member shall not receive both the Council remuneration and the salary from his other position at the same time.

In case a member's salary exceeds his remuneration in the Council, the Council shall pay the member the difference. If the members' position provides him with greater benefits than those provided by the Council, the member shall continue to receive them.

Article 4
As an exception to Article 2 of these bylaws, the member has forty five-day periods as an annual leave, and the chairman decides when the member can take it. Absences on leave must now jeopardise the required number for effectiveness of the Council's meetings.

Article 5
A member should be impartial and objective in all his functions at the Council. He shall not raise during the Council private or personal issues or any issue contrary to the public interest.

Article 6
A member shall attend sessions and committee meetings regularly. He shall also notify the Chairman of the Council or a committee chairman in writing the event of he is not being able to attend a Council session or a committee meeting. Moreover, he shall not leave a session or a meeting before adjournment without permission from the Chairman.

Financial and Personnel Affairs

Article 1
The Council fiscal year is the same as that of the state.

Article 2
The Shura Council shall prepare a draft of the Council annual budget and forward it to the King for approval.

Article 3
The Council budget shall be deposited with the Saudi Arabian Monetary Agency, and withdrawal therefrom shall be against the signature of the Chairman or his Deputy.

Article 4
In case the Council's budget does not cover all Council expenditure, or an unforeseen expense arises, the Chairman shall forward a

memorandum for the required additional funds to the King for approval.

Article 5
Remuneration for titles and grades of positions at the Council shall be determined in the budget and may be modified during the fiscal year by a decision of the Chairman.

Article 6
14th and 15th grade positions shall be filled by royal consent while other positions shall be filled according to law and by-laws of the Civil Service with exemption from competition.

Article 7
The steering committee of the Council shall set rules for the remuneration of non-members who render the Council service, be they government officials or others. As far as remuneration is concerned these rules shall be issued by a decision from the Chairman of the Council.

Article 8
The Shura Council shall not be audited by any other body but within the administrative structure of the Council; there shall be an accounting department. The Steering Committee of the Council shall undertake the auditing. The Chairman may assign a financial or administrative expert to write a report on any of the Council's financial or administrative affairs.

Article 9
At the end of the fiscal year, the General Secretariat shall prepare the final statement of accounts, and the chairman of the Council shall forward it to the King for approval.

Article 10
Without contravention of these by-laws, the Council shall follow the rules pertaining to the accounts of ministers and government agencies to regulate the Council's financial affairs.

Rules and Procedures for Investigation and Trial of Shura Council Members

Article 1
If a member of the Shura Council neglects any of the duties of his work, one of the following actions shall be taken against him:
A written reprimand shall be directed to him.
He shall be fined one month's salary.
His membership shall be terminated

Article 2
A committee of three Council members selected by the Council Chairman shall conduct the investigation.

Article 3
The committee shall inform the member concerned of the alleged misconduct. The committee shall also record his rebuttal in the proceedings of the investigation. The committee shall then report its verdict to the Steering Committee of the Council.

Article 4
The Steering Committee may also form a three-member committee, excluding the Chairman and his Deputy, to investigate the alleged misconduct of the given member. This committee shall be entitled to apply the penalty or a written reprimand or a fine of one month's salary.

If the committee concludes that the member should be expelled, the verdict shall be referred to the Council Chairman, who shall in turn, refer it to the King.

Article 5
The application any of the above penalties does not preclude the initiation of public or private claims against the member.

Appendix 3

The Questionnaire

In The Name Of Allah Most Gracious, Most Merciful

Dear Citizen:

Welcome to the Emirate of Riyadh province.

Praise be to Allah, Saudi Arabia is governed by the greatness of Islam, providing security as well as prosperity. An Islamic gift to us is the rule of the Qur'an and Sunnah. This is accomplished by our country's leaders, specifically Custodian of the Two Holy Mosques and his hardworking Crown Prince, who receive citizens in the Open Councils to help solve their difficulties. Allah has given us a great gift by giving us rulers who do their best to fairly rule the land and help the people.

My dear citizen, I am doing an MA dissertation, concerning the Open Councils, and I would be most grateful if you would answer the following questions.

Your Brother

Faisal Mish'al bin Sa'ud

Q: What Is The Complaint's / The Problem's Type?

Tribal   Properties   Confidential or Familial

Civil / Criminal   Municipal   Hygienic   Governmental

Judicial   A Complaint   Financial (Debts)   Other

Q: Why do you come to the Council instead of resorting to other specialised parties?
....
....

Q: Have you / Do you come across any obstacles when you endeavoured to reach the Council?
Yes   No

Q: How many times have you attended it?
Once   More than once (The number)

What do you think about the decisions taken by it?
Just   Accepted   Oppressive (Why?)

Q: What is your degree of satisfaction?
Excellent   Good   Satisfactory   Dissatisfied

Q: If you did not obtain a convincing solution, what would you choose?
The Judiciary   Other Institutions   Repeating
                                                   the complaint procedure

Others (clarify): ....

The Open Councils

Q: Are you capable of easy access to the King?
Yes   Sometimes   No (Why?)

Q: Do you need an appointment to meet the King or leaders?
Yes   No

Q: Do you find an instant solution to your problem?
Yes   From time to time   No (Why?)

Q: Would you like to meet the officials personally or do you prefer someone else to overcome your difficulty instead of you?
Myself   Another

Q: What do you think of the Open Councils within your country? What do you suggest about this point?
Very Good   Good   Satisfactory   Acceptable
Others: ....

· Suggestions:
1. ....
2. ....
3. ....

Peace Be Upon You

Name: (Not Necessary)   Age:

Appendix 4

The Law of the Provinces

No. A92
Dated 27/08/1412H

With the help of Allah, We, Fahd bin 'Abdul-'Aziz Al Sa'ud, King of the Kingdom of Saudi Arabia, having taken into consideration public interest and the wish to improve the standard of Government Institutions' performance and modernisation in various provinces, have ordered the following:
A. The promulgation of the Law of the Provinces in the attached form

B. That this law shall come into force within a period not exceeding one year effective from the date of its publication

C. That this law shall be published in the Official Gazette (*Umm Al-Qura*)

The Law of the Provinces

Article 1
The aim of this law is to improve the standard of the administrative work and the development in the provinces of the Kingdom. It is also aimed at maintaining security and order, and guaranteeing citizens' rights and freedom within the framework of the Shari'a.

Article 2
The provinces of the Kingdom and governmental seat of each province shall be formed according to a Royal Decree upon the recommendation of the Interior Minister.

Article 3
Administratively, every province shall consist of a number of governorates (of Class A or Class B), districts and centres (of Class A or Class B). Full consideration shall be given to the factors of demography, geography, security, environment and communications. The organisation of a governorate shall be carried out according to a royal decree upon the recommendation of the Interior Minister. Establishment of an affiliation of districts and centres shall take effect upon the Interior Minister's decision, as proposed by the Emir of the province. (As amended by the Royal Decree A/21, dated 30/3/1414H).

Article 4
For each province, an Emir with the rank of minister shall be appointed. A deputy at the highest rank shall assist the Emir and deputise for him during periods of absence. The appointment and the relief of the Emir and his Deputy shall be made by Royal Decree upon the recommendation of the Minister of the Interior.

Article 5
The Emir of the Province shall be answerable to the Interior Minister.

Article 6
An Emir and his Deputy, prior to assuming their duties, shall take the following oath before the King:

"In the name of Allah Almighty, I swear that I will be loyal to my religion then to my King and Country, will not reveal any of the State's

secrets and will protect its interests and laws. I will perform my work in honesty, trust, sincerity and fairness."
Article 7
Every Emir shall assure the administration of the region according to the general policy of the State in compliance with provisions of this Law and other laws and regulations. In particular, he is expected to do the following:
- Maintain security, order and stability, and take necessary measures in accordance with this law and other laws and regulations,
- Implement rulings of the courts upon acquiring their final positions,
- Guarantee human rights and freedom, refrain from any action which affects such rights and freedoms except within the limits provided by the Shari'a and the law,
- Work for social and economic development and public works of the province,
- Work for the development and improvement of public services in the province,
- Administer governorates, districts and centres, and supervise governors, directors of districts and heads of centres, and ascertain their capabilities to perform assigned duties,
- Protect State property and assets, and prevent their usurpation,
- Supervise governmental institutions and their employees in the province and ensure proper performance of their work in honesty and loyalty with consideration of their affiliation with various ministries and service,
- Have direct contact with ministers and heads of agencies to discuss affairs of the province and improve the performance of affiliated institutions and to advise the Minister of the Interior accordingly,
- Submit annual reports to the Minister of the Interior on the efficiency of public services and other affairs of the province as defined by the executive provisions of this law. (As amended by the Royal Decree A/21, dated 30/3/1414H).

Article 8
An annual meeting, attended by Emirs of provinces and presided over the Interior Minister, shall be held to discuss the affairs of the provinces. A report to this effect shall be forwarded to the Prime Minister by the Interior Minister.

Article 9
At least two meetings shall be held every year for Governors and Directors of districts to discuss affairs of the province. The meeting

shall be presided over by the Emir, who shall submit a report to the Interior Minister. (As amended by the Royal Decree A/21, dated 30/3/1414H

Article 10
i) Upon the recommendation of the Minister of the Interior, one deputy or more with a rank not less than Grade 14 shall be appointed for every province following a decision by the Council of Ministers.

ii) Every Class A governorate shall have a governor with a rank not less than Grade 14. Upon the recommendation of the Interior Minister, he shall be appointed by an order issued by the Prime Minster. The governorate shall have a deputy with a rank not less than Grade 12. He shall be appointed by a decision of the Minister of the Interior upon the recommendation of the Emir of the province.

iii) Every Class B governorate shall have a governor with a rank not less than Grade 8. He shall be appointed by a decision of the Minister of the Interior upon the recommendation of the Emir of the Province.

iv) Every Class A district shall have a director with a rank of not less than Grade 5. He shall be appointed by a decision of the Minister of the Interior upon the recommendation of the governor.

Article 11
Emirs of provinces, Governors of governorates and Directors of districts shall reside in their work areas. They shall not be allowed to leave without permission from their direct superiors.

Article 12
The Governors, Directors of districts and heads of centres shall assume their responsibilities within their jurisdictions and within the assigned limits of their powers.

Article 13
Governors shall manage their governorates within their limits of powers as provided in Article 7, excluding clauses (f), (i) and (j). They shall supervise the work of subordinate directors and heads of centres, and ascertain their ability to perform their duties. They shall provide the Emir of the Province with periodic reports about the efficiency of public services ad other affairs of their governorates, as defined by the Executive Regulations of this law.

Article 14
Every ministry or governmental organisation, having services in a province, shall appoint for its organisation in the province, a director with a rank not less than Grade 12. He shall be directly affiliated with

the central institution, and co-ordinate his work with the Emir of the Province.

Article 15

A council, called the Council of the Province, shall be established at every provincial seat.

Article 16

The council of a province shall be composed of:

i) The Emir of the province as chairman of the council,
ii) The Deputy Emir of the Province as vice-chairman of the council,
iii) The Deputy of the governmental seat,
iv) Head of governmental institutions in the province as specified by a resolution to be issued by the Prime Minister upon the recommendation of the Minister of the Interior.
v) A minimum of ten men of knowledge, expertise and specialisation to be appointed from among the inhabitants by an order issued by the Prime Minister after their nomination by the emir of the province and the approval by the Minister of the Interior. Their terms of office shall be four years and shall be renewable.

Article 17

It is stipulated that every member of the Council shall be:

i) A Saudi national by birth and descent,
ii) A person well-known for righteousness and capability
iii) Not younger than 30 years of age
iv) A resident of the province.

Article 18

A member shall be entitled to submit written proposals to the head of the provincial council on matters pertaining to the Council's jurisdiction. Every proposal shall be listed by the Chairman on the Council's agenda for consideration.

Article 19

A member shall not attend discussions of the (provincial) council or its committees if the subject of discussion might concern his personal gain or might benefit individuals for whom his testimony is not acceptable, or individuals who have appointed him as guardian, proxy or representative.

Article 20

A Provincial Council member who wishes to resign shall submit his request to the Minister of the Interior through the Emir of the province.

The Open Councils

His resignation shall not be considered valid until it is approved by the Prime Minister upon a proposal of the Minister of the Interior.

Article 21

In cases other than those mentioned in the Law, an appointed (Provincial Council) member may not be dismissed during the term of his membership without the Prime Minister's order after a proposal of the Minister of the Interior.

When the place of any appointed (Provincial Council) member has become vacant for any reason, a successor shall be appointed within three months, effective from the beginning of vacancy. The term of the new member shall be equal to the remaining period of his predecessor's term in accordance with Article 16, Clause (e) of this law.

Article 23

The Provincial Council shall consider whatever might improve the standard of services in the province, particularly:

i) Defining the needs of the province and proposing their inclusion in the State's Development Plan,

ii) Defining useful projects and putting them in an order of priority, and proposing their endorsement in the annual budget of the State,

iii) Studying urban plans for villages and towns of the province, and following up and co-ordinating the implementation of all allocations to the province from the development plan and the budget,

Article 24

The council of a province shall propose any work needed for the public interest of the population of the province, encourage citizens to participate in that work and submit the proposal to the Minister of the Interior.

Article 25

A Provincial Council is prohibited from considering any topic outside its jurisdiction as provided by terms of this law. Its decisions shall be null and void if its powers are misused. The Minister of the Interior shall issue a decision to this effect.

Article 26

The Provincial Council shall convene every three months in ordinary sessions upon invitation by its Chairman. If he considers it necessary, the Chairman is entitled to summon the Council to extraordinary sessions. The session shall include one or more meetings that are held upon a single summons. The session may not be adjourned until all issues on the agenda are taken into consideration and discussed.

Article 27
Those members who are mentioned in Article 16, Clauses (c) and (d) of this Law must attend meetings of the Provincial Council as part of their official duties. They should attend in person or appoint substitutes when they cannot attend. Regarding members mentioned in Clause (e) of the said Article, unexcused non-attendance at two successive sessions by a member shall be grounds for his dismissal from the Council. In this case, he shall not be re-appointed before two years have elapsed effective from the date of the decision for dismissal.

Article 28
Meetings of a Provincial Council shall not be official unless at least two thirds of its members are present. Its resolutions shall be adopted by an absolute majority or votes of the council's members. In case of a tie vote, the Chairman shall cast the deciding vote.

Article 29
A Provincial Council, in case of need, may form special committees to consider any topics within its powers. It may seek the assistance of experienced people and specialists. It may also invite others to attend the Council's meetings and participate in discussions without having the right to vote.

Article 30
The Minister of the Interior may invite a council to convene under his chairmanship anywhere he deems suitable. He may chair any meeting he attends.

Article 31
A Provincial Council may not convene without an invitation its Chairman or his Deputy, or without an order issued by the Minister of the Interior.

Article 32
The Chairman of a council shall submit a copy of the resolution to the Minister of the Interior.

Article 33
The Chairman of a Provincial Council shall inform ministries and governmental services of any resolutions concerning them, which are passed by the council.

Article 34
Ministries and governmental institutions shall take into consideration resolutions passed by a Provincial Council in accordance with provisions of Article 23, Clauses (a) and (b) of this law. If a ministry or a governmental institution does not agree to consider one of these

resolutions, it shall explain the reasons to the Provincial Council. In case of dissatisfaction, the Council shall refer the matter to the Minister of the Interior for reconsideration by the Prime Minister.

Article 35
Every ministry or institution with services in a province shall immediately inform the Provincial Council of projects, which were decided upon in the budget for the province, together with its allocations from the development plan.

Article 36
Any minister or head of institution may seek the opinion of a Provincial Council on matters pertaining to his jurisdiction in the province. The Council shall forward its opinion in this regard.

Article 37
The Council of Ministers, upon a proposal of the Minister of the Interior, shall set the remuneration of the Chairman of a Provincial Council and its members, taking into account the cost of transportation and accommodation.

A Provincial Council can be dissolved only on an order by the Prime Minister, following the recommendation of the Minister of the Interior. New members shall be appointed within three months effective form the date of the dissolution. During the period, members mentioned in Article 16, Clauses (c) and (d) of this law, shall perform the duties of the Council under chairmanship of the Emir of the province.

Article 39
A secretariat for a Provincial Council shall be set up at the governmental seat of the province to prepare its agenda, send timely invitations, record discussions carried out during the sessions, count votes, prepare the minutes of sessions, draft decisions and perform necessary work for the monitoring of the council's session and the registration of all decisions.

Article 40
The Minister of the Interior shall issue the necessary regulations to implement this law.

Appendix 5

The Basic Law of Government

N: A/90
Dated : 27th Sha'ban 1412 AH (1992 AD)

With the help of Allah, We, Fahd bin 'Abdul-'Aziz Al Sa'ud, Monarch of the Kingdom of Saudi Arabia, having taken into consideration the public interest, and in view of the progress of the State in various fields and out of the desire to achieve the objectives we are pursuing, having decreed the following:

A. The promulgation of the Basic Law of Government as the attached text

B. That all regulations, orders and decrees in force shall remain valid when this Basic Law comes into force, until they are amended to conform with it

C. That this decree shall be published in the Official Gazette (*Umm Al-Qura*), and shall come into force on the date of its publication.

In the name of Allah, the Most Compassionate the Most Merciful:

The Basic Law of Government
Chapter One
General Principles

Article 1
The Kingdom of Saudi Arabia is a sovereign Arab Islamic State. Its religion is Islam. Its constitution is Almighty Allah's Book, the Holy Qur'an, and the Sunnah (tradition) of the Prophet (PBUH). Arabic is the language of the Kingdom. The city of Riyadh is the capital.

Article 2
The State's public holidays are Eid Al-Fitr (the Feast of Ramadan) and Eid Al-Adha (The Feast of the Sacrifice). Its calendar follows the Hijri year (the lunar year).

Article 3
The flag of the State is as follows:
i) Its colour is green.
ii) Its width equals two thirds of its length.
iii) The words, "There is no Allah but Allah and Muhammad is His Messenger" are inscribed in the centre, with a drawn sword underneath. The flag should never be inverted.
The law will specify the rules pertaining to the flag.

Article 4
The State's emblem represents two crossed swords with a palm tree in the middle of the upper space between them. The law will define the State's anthem and medals.

Chapter Two
The Law of Government

Article 5
i) Monarchy is the system of rule in the Kingdom of Saudi Arabia.
ii) The rulers of the country shall be taken from amongst the sons of the founder King 'Abdul-'Aziz Bin 'Abdul-Rahman al Faisal Al-Sa'ud, and their descendants. The most upright among them shall receive allegiance according to Almighty Allah's Book and His Messenger's Sunnah (The Tradition).
iii) The King shall choose the Crown Prince and relieve him of his duties by a Royal Decree.
iv) The Crown Prince shall devote himself exclusively to his duties as Crown Prince and shall perform any other duties delegated to him by the King.
v) Upon the death of the King, the Crown Prince shall assume the Royal powers until a pledge of allegiance (*bay'a*) is given.

Article 6
In support of the Book of Allah and the Sunnah of His Messenger, citizens shall give the pledge of allegiance (*bay'a*) to the King, professing loyalty in times of hardship and ease.

Article 7
Government in the Kingdom of Saudi Arabia derives its authority from the Book of Allah and the Sunnah of the Prophet, which are the ultimate sources of reference for this Law and the other laws of the State.

Article 8
Government in the Kingdom of Saudi Arabia is based on justice, Shura (consultation) and equality according to Islamic Shari'a.

Chapter Three
The Values of Saudi Society

Article 9
The family is the nucleus of Saudi society. Members of the family shall be raised in the Islamic creed, which demands allegiance and obedience to Allah, to His Prophet and to the rulers, respect for and obedience to the laws, and love for and pride in the homeland and its glorious history.

Article 10
The state shall aspire to promote family bonds and Arab-Islamic values. It shall take care of all individuals and provide the right conditions for the growth of their talents and skills.

Article 11
Saudi Society is based on full adherence to Allah's guidance. Members of this society shall co-operate amongst themselves in charity, piety and cohesion.

Article 12
Consolidation of the national unity is a duty. The State shall forbid all activities that may lead to division, disorder and partition.

Article 13
The aim of education is to implant the Islamic creed in the hearts of all youths, to help them acquire knowledge and skills, to qualify them to become useful members of their society, to love their homeland and take pride in its history.

Economic Principles

Article 14
All natural resources that Allah has deposited underground, above ground, in territorial waters or within the land and sea domains under the authority of the State, together with revenues of these resources, shall be the property of the State, as provided by the Law.
The law shall specify means for exploitation, protection and development of these resources in the best interest of the State and its security and economy.

Article 15
No concessions or licenses to exploit any public resources of the State shall be granted unless authorised by provisions of the law.

Article 16
Public funds are inviolable. They shall be protected by the State and safeguarded by all citizens and residents.

Article 17
Ownership, capital and labour are basic components of the economic and social entity of the Kingdom. They are personal rights that perform a social function in accordance with the Islamic Shari'a.

Article 18
The State shall guarantee private ownership and its sanctity. No one shall be deprived of his private property, unless in service of the public interest. In this case, fair compensation shall be given to him.

Article 19
General confiscation of assets is prohibited. No confiscation of an individual's assets shall be enforced without a judicial ruling.

Article 20
No taxes or fees shall be imposed, except in need and on a just basis. Imposition, amendment, cancellation or exemption shall take place according to the provisions of the law.

Article 21
Zakat shall be collected and spent for legitimate expenses.

Article 22
Economic and social development shall be carried out according to a fair and wise plan.

Chapter Five
Rights and Duties

Article 23
The State shall protect the Islamic creed, apply the Shari'a, encourage good and discourage evil, and undertake its duty regarding the propagation of Islam (*da'wa*).

Article 24
The State shall develop and maintain the two holy mosques. It shall provide care and security to pilgrims to help them perform their Hajj and 'Umrah and to visit to the Prophet's Mosque in ease and comfort.

Article 25
The State will nourish the aspirations of Arab and Muslim nations in solidarity and harmony and strengthen relations with friendly states.

Article 26
The State shall protect human rights in accordance with the Shari'a.

Article 27
The State shall guarantee the rights of the citizens and their families in cases of emergency, illness, disability and old age. The State shall support the Social Insurance Law and encourage organisations and individuals to participate in philanthropic activities.

Article 28
The State shall facilitate job opportunities for every able person, and enact laws to protect the worker and the employer.

Article 29
The State shall patronise sciences, letters and culture. It shall encourage scientific research, protect Islamic and Arab heritage and contribute towards Arab, Islamic and human civilisation.

Article 30
The State shall provide public education and commit itself to the eradication of illiteracy.

Article 31
The State shall look after public health and provide health care for every citizen.

Article 32
The State shall work towards the preservation, protection and improvement of the environment, as well as prevent pollution.

Article 33
The State shall form armed forces and equip them to defend the Islamic creed, the two Holy Mosques, society and the homeland.

Article 34
It shall be the duty of every citizen to defend the Islamic creed, society and homeland. The law shall specify rules for military service.

Article 35
The law shall specify rules pertaining to Saudi Arabian nationality.

Article 36
The State shall provide security for all citizens and residents on its territories. No one may be confined, arrested or imprisoned without reference to the law.

Article 37
Dwellings are inviolable. Access is prohibited without their owners' permissions. No search may be made except in cases specified by the law.

Article 38
No one shall be punished for another's crimes. No conviction or penalty shall be inflicted without reference to the Shari'a or the provisions of the law. Punishment shall not be imposed ex post facto.

Article 39
The mass media and all other vehicles of expression shall employ civil and polite language, contribute towards the education of the nation and strengthen unity. It is prohibited to commit acts leading to disorder and

division, affecting the security of the state and its public relations, or undermining human dignity and rights. Details shall be specified in the law.

Article 40
The privacy of telegraphic and postal communications, and telephone and other means of communication shall be inviolate. There shall be no confiscation, delay surveillance or eavesdropping, except in cases provided by the law.

Article 41
Residents in the Kingdom of Saudi Arabia shall abide by its laws; observe the values of the Saudi community and respect Saudi traditions and feelings.

Article 42
The State shall grant the right of political asylum provided it is in the public interest. International agreements and laws shall define rules and procedures for the extradition of common criminals.

Article 43
Councils held by the King and the Crown Prince shall be open for all citizens and anyone else who may have a complaint or a grievance. A citizen shall be entitled to address public authorities and discuss any matters of concern to him.

Chapter Six
The Authority of the State

Article 44
The Authorities of the State consist of:
- The Judicial Authority.
- The Executive Authority.
- The Regulatory Authority.

These authorities will co-operate in the performance of their functions, according to this Law or other laws. The King is the ultimate arbiter for these authorities.

Article 45
The Holy Qur'an and the Sunnah (tradition) of Allah's Messenger shall be the source for fatwas (religious advisory rulings). The Law shall specify hierarchical organisation for the composition of the Council of the Senior 'Ulama, the Research Administration and the Office of the Mufti, together with their functions.

Article 46
The Judiciary is an independent authority. The decisions of judges shall not be subject to any authority other than the authority of the Islamic Shari'a.

Article 47
All people, either citizens or residents in the Kingdom, are entitled to file suits on an equal basis. The law shall specify procedures for this purpose.

Article 48
The courts shall apply rules of the Islamic Shari'a in cases that are brought before them, according to the Holy Qur'an and the Sunnah, and according to laws which are decreed by the ruler in agreement with the Holy Qur'an and the Sunnah.

Article 49
Courts are empowered to arbitrate in all disputes and crimes, taking into account the provision of Article 53 of this law.

Article 50
The King or whomsoever he may deputise shall concern himself with the implementation of judicial rulings.

Article 51
The law shall specify the composition of the Supreme Judiciary Council and its functions, as well as the hierarchy for the courts and their functions.

Article 52
Judges shall be appointed and relieved by Royal Decree, based on a proposal of the Supreme Judiciary Council, in accordance with provisions of the law.

Article 53
The law shall specify the hierarchy of the Board of Grievances and its functions.

Article 54
The law shall specify the relationship between the Commission of Inquiry and the Attorney General and their organisation and functions.

Article 55
The King shall rule the nation according to the Shari'a. He shall also supervise the implementation of the Shari'a, the general policy of the State and the defence and protection of the country.

Article 56
The King is the Prime Minister. Members of the Council of Ministers shall assist him in the performance of his mission according to the

provisions of this law and other laws. The Council of Ministers law shall specify the powers of the Council in respect of internal and external affairs, organisation of governmental departments and their co-ordination. In addition, the law shall specify the qualifications and the powers of the ministers, ministerial accountability procedures and all matters pertaining to the ministers. The law of the Council of Ministers and the areas of their authority may be amended according to this law.

Article 57
i) The King shall appoint and relieve deputies of the Prime Minister and member ministers of the Council by Royal Decree.
ii) Deputies of the Prime Minister and member ministers of the Council shall be jointly responsible to the King for the implementation of the Shari'a, laws and the general policy of the State.
iii) The King is entitled to dissolve and reconstitute the Council of Ministers.

Article 58
The King shall appoint those of ministerial rank, deputy ministers, and those who are at the highest grade and relieve them by a Royal Decree as provided by the Law. Ministers and heads of independent departments shall be answerable to the King in respect of the miniteries and agencies they head.

Article 59
The law shall specify the rules of the Civil Service, including salaries, awards, compensations, privileges and pensions.

Article 60
The King is the Supreme Commander of the Armed Forces. He shall appoint and dismiss officers from service, as provided by terms of the law.

Article 61
The King shall announce any state of emergency or general mobilisation and shall declare war. The law shall specify rules for this purpose.

Article 62
If an imminent danger is threatening the safety of the Kingdom, the integrity of its territories or the security and interests of its people, or is impeding the functions of official organisations, the King may take urgent measures to deal with such a danger. When he considers that these measures should continue, necessary arrangements shall be made in accordance with the law.

The Open Councils

Article 63
The King shall receive Kings and heads of state, appoint his representatives to other states and receive credentials of other states' representatives accredited to him.

Article 64
The King shall award medals according to provisions of the law.

Article 65
The King may delegate some powers of authority to the Crown Prince by royal decree.

Article 66
Should the King happen to travel abroad, he shall issue a royal decree to deputise the Crown Prince to manage the affairs of State and look after the interests of the people, as set out in the royal decree.

Article 67
The Regulatory Authority shall be concerned with the making of laws and regulations, which will safeguard all interests, and remove evil from the states affairs, according to Shari'a. Its powers shall be exercised according to provisions of this law and the law of the Council of Ministers and the Law of the Shura Council.

Article 68
The Shura Council shall be established. Its law shall specify the details of its formation, powers and selection of members. The King may dissolve and reconstitute the Shura Council.

Article 69
The King may summon the Shura Council and the Council of Ministers for a joint session. He may summon others whom he deems necessary to attend the meeting and discuss whatever affairs he considers fit.

Article 70
Laws, international agreements, treaties and concessions shall be approved and amended by royal decrees.

Article 71
Laws shall be published in the Official Gazette (*Umm Al-Qura*), and implemented effective from the date of publication, unless another date is specified.

Chapter Seven
Financial Affairs

Article 72
i) The Law shall include provisions for the State's revenues and their depositing with the General Treasury of the State.

ii) Revenues shall be recorded and spent according to procedures stipulated by provisions of the law.
Article 73
No commitment to pay a sum of money from the General Treasury shall be made without adherence to budget rules. If provisions of the budget cannot cover the demand, then a provision shall be made through a royal decree.
Article 74
Assets of the State may not be sold, rented or disposed of unless so authorised by the law.
Article 75
Laws shall specify provisions for currency, banks, standards, measures and weights.
Article 76
The law shall set the fiscal year for the State. The budget shall be announced according to a Royal Decree. It shall specify assessed amounts of revenue and expenditure one month ahead of the coming fiscal year. If the budget cannot be issued due to compelling reasons before the beginning of the new fiscal year, the budget of the previous year shall remain in force until the new budget can be issued.
Article 77
The competent department shall prepare the closing account of the State for the past year and forward it to the Prime Minister.
Article 78
Budgets and the closing of accounts of departments that have corporate rights, shall be subject to the same procedures which are applicable to the State's budget and closing accounts.

Chapter Eight
Institutions of Audit

Article 79
All revenues and expenditures of the State, as well as movable and fixed assets, shall be subsequently audited to ensure proper use and management. An annual report to this effect shall be forwarded to the Prime Minister. The law shall specify details of the competent auditing institution, together with its affiliations and areas of authority.
Article 80
Governmental institutions shall also be audited to ensure proper administrative performance and implementation of laws. Financial and

administrative violations shall be investigated. An annual report shall be forwarded to the Prime Minister. The law shall specify details of the competent institution in charge, together with its affiliations and areas of authority.

Chapter Nine
General Principles

Article 81
With regard to treaties and agreements, the application of this Law shall not violate commitments of the Kingdom of Saudi Arabia towards other states, international organisations and bodies.

Article 82
No provision of this Law whatsoever may be suspended except on a temporary basis, such as in wartime or during the declaration of state of emergency. Such a suspension shall be in accordance with the terms of the law and may not violate Article 7.

Article 83
No amendment to this law shall be made, except in the same manner as it was promulgated.

Appendix 6

The Cabinet System

Date: 3/3/1414 AH

With the help of Allah, We, Fahd bin 'Abdul-'Aziz Al-Sa'ud, Monarch of the Kingdom of Saudi Arabia,
After reviewing the Basic Law of Government, issued by Royal Decree No. A/90, dated 27/8/1412 AH,
And having reviewed the law of the Council of Ministers issued by Royal Decree No. 38, dated 22/10/1377AH, and its amendments,
And having reviewed Shura Council Law issued by Royal Decree No. A/91, dated 27/8/1412 AH,
And having reviewed the Royal Decree No. M/23, dated 26/8/1412 AH (1/3/1992 AD), we, Fahd bin 'Abdul-'Aziz Al Sa'ud, King of the Saudi Arabia,
Have decreed the following:

A. The promulgation of the Law of the Council of Ministers as in the attached text,
B. That this law supersedes Council of Ministers Law issued by a Royal Decree No. 38, dated 22/10/1377 AH (25/7/1919 AD), and its amendments,
C. That all regulations, orders and decrees in force shall remain valid when this Council of Ministers Law comes into force until they are amended to conform with it,
D. That this decree shall be published in the Official Gazette (*Umm Al-Qura*) and shall come into force ninety (90) days after the formation of the Shura Council, as stipulated in the first Royal Decree concerning it.

General Principles

Article 1
The Council of Ministers is a regulatory authority and the King is the Prime Minister.

Article 2
The city of Riyadh is the seat of the Council of Ministers. Meetings may also be held in some other locations in the Kingdom.

Article 3
It is stipulated that every member of the Council of Ministers shall be:
i) A Saudi national by birth and descent,
ii) A person well-known for righteousness and capability,
iii) Of good conduct and reputation, not previously convicted for a crime of immorality or dishonour.

Article 4
Prior to the assumption of their duties, the Ministers shall take the following oath before the King:
{I swear by Allah Almighty to be loyal to my religion, then to my King and country. I swear not to reveal any of the State's secrets, to protect its interests and laws, and to perform my duties with sincerity, integrity and fairness}.

Article 5
The office of minister may not be combined with any other government post, unless the need for such an exception arises and the Prime Minister approves it.

Article 6
A cabinet minister may not buy, lease, and rent directly or through a proxy, or by public auction, any of the properties of the State. A

minister also may not sell or offer for rent any of his properties to the government. A minister may not engage in any commercial of financial enterprises. A minister also may not accept board membership in any firm.

Article 7
The Council of Ministers' meetings are presided over by the King, who is the Prime Minister, or by a deputy of the Prime Minister. The resolutions of the Council of Ministers become final after the King's approval.

Article 8
Cabinet ministers are appointed, relieved of their duties and their resignation accepted by Royal decree. Their duties are determined in accordance with Article 57 and 58 of the Basic Law of the Government. The by-laws of the Council of Ministers shall stipulate their rights.

Article 9
The fixed term of the Council of Ministers shall be four years, during which a new council may be formed by Royal Decree. If the term expires before the formation of the new Council, the previous Council shall remain active until the new Council is formed.

Article 10
A minister is the ultimate authority in running the affairs of his ministry, and he carries out his duties in accordance with the ruling of this law as well as other laws and regulations.

Article 11
i) Only a minister shall deputise for another minister in the Council of Ministers and in accordance with a decree issued by the Prime Minister.
ii) A deputy minister shall assume the responsibility of the minister in the latter's absence.

The Formation of the Council

Article 12
The Council of Ministers shall be composed of:
i) A Prime Minister
ii) Deputy Prime Ministers
iii) Ministers with Portfolios
iv) Ministers of State appointed as members of the Council of Ministers by Royal Decree

v) Counsellors of the King, appointed members of the Council of Ministers by Royal Decree

Article 13

The right to attend meetings of the Council of Ministers shall be an exclusive right of its ministers and the Secretary General of the Council of Ministers. At the request of the Prime Minister, or a minister of the Council, and with the approval of the Prime Minister, a state official or an expert shall be permitted to attend the meetings of the Council of Ministers to present information and explanations. The right to vote belongs exclusively to the ministers.

Article 14

Any meeting held by the Council of Ministers shall not be considered official without a quorum of at least two-third of its members. Resolutions shall not be considered official without majority approval. In case of a tie, the Prime Minister shall cast the deciding vote. In exceptional cases, meetings of the Council of Ministers may be considered official with half of the members in attendance. In such cases, resolutions shall not be considered official without the approval of at least two-thirds of the members in attendance. Such exceptional cases will be decided by the Prime Minister.

Article 15

The Council of Ministers shall not pass a resolution relevant to a ministry in the absence of the concerned minister or whoever deputises for him unless it is absolutely necessary.

Article 16

The deliberations of the Council of Ministers are confidential. Resolutions are public except those deemed classified in accordance with a resolution by the Council of Ministers.

Article 17

Ministers of the Council shall be tried for violations committed in carrying out official business in accordance with a special law that specifies the violations, the procedures for prosecution and trial and the formation of courts.

Article 18

The Council of Ministers shall form committees from its members of from others, to study an issue on the agenda of the Council and prepare a special report about it. The by-laws of the Council shall specify the number of committees and the rules of procedure.

The Functions of the Council of Ministers

Article 19
While deferring to provisions of the Basic Law of Government and the Shura Council Law, the cabinet shall draw up the internal, external, financial, economic, educational and defence policies as well as general affairs of the State and shall supervise their implementation. It shall also review the resolutions of the Shura Council. It has the executive power and is the final authority in financial and administrative affairs of all ministries and other government institutions.

Regulatory Affairs

Article 20
While deferring to Shura Council Law, laws, treaties, international agreements and 'concessions' shall be issued and amended by Royal Decrees after deliberations by the Council of Ministers.

Article 21
The Council shall study draft laws and regulations on the agenda and vote on them chapter by chapter and then as a whole in accordance with the bylaws of the Council.

Article 22
Every minister may propose a draft law or regulation related to the work of his ministry. Every member of the Council of Ministers may propose what he deems worthy of discussion in the Council of Ministers' meetings after the approval of the Prime Minister.

Article 23
All laws shall be published in the Official Gazette (*Umm Al-Qura*) and shall be put into force from the date of its publication unless it is stipulated otherwise.

Executive Affairs

Article 24
The Council, being the ultimate executive authority, shall have full jurisdiction over all executive and management affairs. The following shall be included in its executive jurisdiction:
- Monitoring the implementation of regulations, by-laws and resolutions,
- Creating and ranging public institutions,
- Following up implementation of general development,

- Forming committees for the oversight of the ministries' and other governmental agencies' conduct of business. These committees may also investigate any referred matter. The committees shall submit the findings of their investigations within a set time to the Council, and the Council shall consider these findings. It shall have the right to form committees of inquiry accordingly to make a final decision taking into consideration the regulations and stipulations of the by-laws.

Financial Affairs

Article 25
The government shall not contract a loan without the approval of the Council of Ministers and the issue of a Royal Decree.

Article 26
The Council of Ministers shall examine the state budget and vote on each of its chapters. It is then promulgated by Royal Decree.

Article 27
Any supplement to the budget shall only be made by Royal Decree.

Article 28
The Minister of Finance and National Economy shall submit the closing account of the State from the previous fiscal year to the Prime Minister to be referred to the Council of Ministers for approval.

Presidency of the Council of Ministers

Article 29
The King, who is the Prime Minister, undertakes the guidance and supervision of the general policy of the State and secures guidance, co-ordination and co-operation among the various governmental agencies. He ensures harmony, continuity and unity in all functions of the Council of Ministers. He supervises the Council of Ministers, the ministries and government agencies and monitors the implementation of regulations, bylaws and resolutions.

All ministries and other governmental agencies shall submit, within ninety (90) days from the beginning of each fiscal year, a financial report of what has been achieved in comparison with the stipulations of the general plan for development for the previous fiscal year. The report shall cover the difficulties of its implementation and proposals for improvement.

The Administrative Structure of the Council of Ministers

Article 30
The administrative structure of the Council of Ministers shall be comprised of:
- The Office of the Prime Minister.
- The General Secretariat of the Council of Ministers.
- The Commission of Specialists.

The internal charter of the Council of Ministers shall specify the structures of these agencies, their jurisdictions and the manner of the performance of their duties.

Article 31
The bylaws of the Council of Ministers shall be issued by Royal Order.

Article 32
Modification of this law can only be made in the same manner of its issuance.

The Duration of the Ministers

No. A/4
Dated 3/3/1414 AH (21/8/93 AD).

With the help of Allah, We, Fahd bin 'Abdul-'Aziz Al Sa'ud, Monarch of the Kingdom of Saudi Arabia, having reviewed Article 58 of the Basic Law of Government issued by Royal Order No. A/90 and dated 27/8/1412 AH (2/3/1992 AD). Having reviewed the Law of the Ministers and Employees of the Highest Rank (excellent grade) issued by Royal Order No. M/10 dated 1391 AH (1971 AD).

And in accordance with public interest, hereby order the following:

A. The term of office for a minister or an employee of the highest rank (excellent grade) shall not exceed four years, and his service shall terminate at the end of this period unless a royal order for extending it is issued.

B. The term of office for whoever currently occupies the post of minister or a post of the highest rank (excellent grade) shall terminate two years after the issue of this order unless a royal order for its extension is issued for a further period not to exceed two years. Unless a royal order for a further extension at the end of this tenure is issued according to item (1) of this order, the tenure shall terminate.

C. The Deputy Prime Minister and ministers shall implement this order of ours, each in his own jurisdiction.